TEACHER QUALITY

Understanding the Effectiveness of Teacher Attributes

◆

Jennifer King Rice

ECONOMIC POLICY INSTITUTE

About the Author

Jennifer King Rice is Associate Professor in the Department of Education Policy and Leadership at the University of Maryland and Research Associate with the Economic Policy Institute. Her research draws on the discipline of economics to explore education policy questions concerning the efficiency, equity, and adequacy of U.S. public education. Her current work focuses on teachers as a critical resource in the education process, and she is engaged in several projects to study the costs and efficacy of enhancing teacher quality through promising recruitment, retention, and professional development strategies. Her research has been published in numerous journals including *Educational Evaluation and Policy Analysis, Economics of Education Review, Educational Policy, Education Administration Quarterly,* and *The Journal of Education Finance* as well as multiple edited volumes including several recent yearbooks of the American Education Finance Association. She is co-editor (with Chris Roellke) of *Fiscal Policy in Urban Education.* She recently completed a post-doctoral fellowship with the National Academy of Education/Spencer Foundation, and is currently a member of the board of directors of the American Education Finance Association. She earned her M.S. and Ph.D. degrees from Cornell University, and prior to joining the faculty at the University of Maryland, was a researcher at Mathematica Policy Research in Washington, D.C.

ECONOMIC POLICY INSTITUTE
1660 L Street, NW, Suite 1200
Washington, D.C. 20036

http://www.epinet.org

ISBN: 1-932066-06-3

Table of contents

Acknowledgments

This book was prepared under contract with the Economic Policy Institute. It is based on a paper originally prepared for presentation at the 1999 American Educational Research Association Conference in Montreal, Canada. Revisions to the original work were supported through a postdoctoral fellowship with the National Academy of Education and the Spencer Foundation. The author would like to thank Ira Steinberg and Bud Rorison for their assistance with the literature review, and Richard Rothstein, Larry Mishel, Doug Harris, Chris Roellke, David Monk, Bill Fowler, Whitney Allgood, Michael Allen, Dan Goldhaber, and Anne Heald for their valuable comments on early drafts. The author also acknowledges the editorial assistance provided by Lisa Goffredi and Joseph Procopio. The author assumes responsibility for any remaining errors or omissions.

Other books from the Economic Policy Institute

Inequality at the Starting Gate: Social Background Differences in Achievement as Children Begin School

School Vouchers:
Examining the Evidence

The Class Size Debate

Can Public Schools Learn From Private Schools?

Where's the Money Gone?
Changes in the Level and Composition of Education Spending

Risky Business:
Private Management of Public Schools

School Choice:
Examining the Evidence

Executive summary

Teacher quality matters. In fact, it is the most important school-related factor influencing student achievement. Moreover, teacher compensation represents a significant public investment: in 2002 alone, the United States invested $192 billion in teacher pay and benefits. Given the size of this investment, there is remarkably little research to guide such critical decisions as whom to hire, retain, and promote. In the absence of a strong, robust, and deep body of research, the debate in this field is largely ideological.

This analysis reviews a wide range of empirical studies that examine the impact of teacher characteristics on teacher effectiveness in order to draw conclusions about the extent to which these characteristics are, in fact, linked with teacher performance. Greater clarity on the empirical evidence can inform the wisdom of current practice, guide state efforts as they struggle with *No Child Left Behind* compliance regarding teacher quality, and provide direction for future teacher policy decisions. For example, developing an approach to policy that values different and multiple teacher characteristics based on the research evidence may prove promising. It is important to note that many personal characteristics important for a good teacher are not measured in the studies reviewed. The focus is on aspects of teacher background that can be translated into policy recommendations and incorporated into teaching practice.

The framework for this study includes five broad categories of measurable and policy-relevant indicators to organize the teacher characteristics assumed to reflect teacher quality. It is notable that findings for these characteristics frequently differ for teachers at the elementary school level and teachers at the high school level and that the body of research on the subject of teacher quality suggests that the context of teaching matters (e.g., differences in grade levels, subject areas, and student populations). A refined understanding of how teacher attributes affect their performance across these different teaching contexts can be helpful in determining the range of potentially effective policy options.

The highlights of the empirical evidence include:

Teacher experience
- Several studies have found a positive effect of experience on teacher

effectiveness; specifically, the "learning by doing" effect is most obvious in the early years of teaching.

Teacher preparation programs and degrees

- Research suggests that the selectivity/prestige of the institution a teacher attended has a positive effect on student achievement, particularly at the secondary level. This may partially be a reflection of the cognitive ability of the teacher.
- Evidence suggests that teachers who have earned advanced degrees have a positive impact on high school mathematics and science achievement when the degrees earned were in these subjects.
- Evidence regarding the impact of advanced degrees at the elementary level is mixed.

Teacher certification

- Research has demonstrated a positive effect of certified teachers on high school mathematics achievement when the certification is in mathematics.
- Studies show little clear impact of emergency or alternative-route certification on student performance in either mathematics or science, as compared to teachers who acquire standard certification.

Teacher coursework

- Teacher coursework in both the subject area taught and pedagogy contributes to positive education outcomes.
- Pedagogical coursework seems to contribute to teacher effectiveness at all grade levels, particularly when coupled with content knowledge.
- The importance of content coursework is most pronounced at the high school level.
- While the studies on the field experience component of teacher education are not designed to reveal causal relationships, they suggest positive effects in terms of opportunity to learn the profession and reduced anxiety among new teachers.

Teachers' own test scores

- Tests that assess the literacy levels or verbal abilities of teachers have been shown to be associated with higher levels of student achievement.
- Studies show the National Teachers Examination and other state-mandated tests of basic skills and/or teaching abilities are less consistent predictors of teacher performance.

Given that many dimensions of teacher characteristics matter—preparation in both pedagogic and subject content, credentials, experience, and test scores—the findings from the literature imply that there is no merit in large-scale elimination of all credentialing requirements. Nor are improvements in teacher quality likely to be realized through the status quo. Rather, teacher policies need to reflect the reality that teaching is a complex activity that is influenced by the many elements of teacher quality. Most of the research does not seek to capture interactions among the multiple dimensions of teacher quality, and as a result, there are major gaps in the research that still need to be explored. Nor does the research fully address evidence about teacher quality at the elementary and middle school levels, in subjects other than mathematics, or among different populations of students (such as high poverty, English language learners, or special education).

In opposition to those who propose to eliminate all requirements for entering the teaching profession, this analysis supports a judicious use of the research evidence on teacher characteristics and teacher effectiveness. The evidence indicates that neither an extreme centralized bureaucratization nor a complete deregulation of teacher requirements is a wise approach for improving teacher quality. What holds a great deal more promise is refining the policies and practices employed to build a qualified body of teachers in elementary schools, middle schools, and high schools; for disadvantaged, special needs, and advantaged students; and for math, science, languages, English, social studies, and the arts.

Education policy makers and administrators would be well served by recognizing the complexity of the issue and adopting multiple measures along many dimensions to support existing teachers and to attract and hire new, highly qualified teachers. The research suggests that investing in teachers can make a difference in student achievement. In order to implement needed policies associated with staffing every classroom—even the most challenging ones—with high-quality teachers, substantial and targeted investments must first be made in both teacher quality and education research.

CHAPTER 1

Introduction:
The policy and research context

Are qualified teachers really quality teachers? Likewise, are hiring and compensation policies that reward certain qualifications the equivalent of investing in teacher quality? Does hiring and retaining qualified teachers lead to improvements in student achievement? Researchers and policy makers agree that teacher quality is a pivotal policy issue in education reform, particularly given the proportion of education dollars devoted to teacher compensation coupled with the evidence that teachers are the most important school-related factor affecting student achievement. However, considerable disagreement surrounds what specific teacher attributes indicate quality and how to better invest resources to provide quality teachers for all students. This review examines empirical evidence on the relationship between teacher attributes and teacher effectiveness with the goal of informing federal, state, and local teacher policy.

The policy context

Education is the compilation and product of many and varied resources. Among these, teachers stand out as a key to realizing the high standards that are increasingly emphasized in schools and school systems across the country. Despite general agreement about the importance of high-quality teachers, researchers, practitioners, policy makers, and the public have been unable to reach a consensus about what specific qualities and characteristics make a good teacher. Even more concerning is the array of policy statements regarding teacher preparation that have been set forth in the face of volumes of inconclusive and inconsistent evidence about what teacher attributes really contribute to desired educational outcomes. Policy makers are left with questions surrounding what counts as a quality teacher—information that could be valuable in guiding policies regarding whom to hire, whom to reward, and how best to distribute teachers across schools and classrooms. Answers to these questions have potentially important implications for the efficiency and equity of public education.

The intense interest in teacher policy is motivated by several compelling factors. One factor relates to the high proportion of educational dollars devoted to teacher compensation. The single largest category of educational spending is devoted to the purchase of teacher time. A substantial portion of the 1999-2000 national investment in public education, which totaled over $360 billion, was used to employ almost 2.9 million teachers to educate more than 46 million public elementary and secondary students (National Center for Education Statistics 2000).[1] Guthrie and Rothstein (1998) assert that teacher salaries account for at least 50% of typical school district expenditures. Further, in their analysis of spending in the New York City public school system, Speakman et al. (1996) found that over 41% of the total expenditures in this district were devoted to the salaries and benefits of instructional teachers. An additional 6% was spent on other instructional personnel such as substitutes and paraprofessionals. This high level of investment mirrors the general sentiment among policy makers, researchers, and the general public that teachers are perhaps the most valuable resource allocated to student education.

Further, the enhancement of teacher quality is likely to be quite costly. Increases in teacher salaries, incentives such as loan-forgiveness programs, heightened teacher preparation requirements, and other efforts to prepare, recruit, and retain high-quality teachers are all associated with substantial costs. These costs could be managed by targeting specific areas of need where teacher shortages are most pronounced, such as particular subject areas (e.g., mathematics and science), types of classrooms (e.g., special education), and geographic areas (e.g., urban settings). Nevertheless, a clear sense of which teacher attributes really lead to improved educational outcomes should guide these important investment decisions, particularly given the many competing policy options to enhance teacher quality, as well as other attractive education policy proposals. In a context of limited resources, difficult policy choices must be made, and solid evidence should be used to guide those decisions.

The willingness of policy makers and taxpayers to devote such a large proportion of education dollars to teachers highlights the undisputed importance of teachers in realizing educational goals. A number of researchers have argued that teacher quality is a powerful predictor of student performance. In her analysis of teacher preparation and student achievement across states, Darling-Hammond (2000) reports that "measures of teacher preparation and certification are by far the strongest correlates of student achievement in reading and mathematics, both before and after controlling for student poverty and language status." She contends that measures of teacher quality are more strongly related to student achievement than other kinds of educational investments such as reduced class size, overall spending on education, and teacher salaries.[2]

In contrast to the approach used by Darling-Hammond, which equates teacher quality with specific qualifications, Rivkin, Hanushek, and Kain (1998) identify teacher quality in terms of student performance outcomes.[3] Their research identifies teacher quality as the most important school-related factor influencing student achievement. They conclude from their analysis of 400,000 students in 3,000 schools that, while school quality is an important determinant of student achievement, the most important predictor is teacher quality. In comparison, class size, teacher education, and teacher experience play a small role.

Hanushek (1992) estimates that the difference between having a good teacher and having a bad teacher can exceed one grade-level equivalent in annual achievement growth. Likewise, Sanders (1998) and Sanders and Rivers (1996) argue that the single most important factor affecting student achievement is teachers, and the effects of teachers on student achievement are both additive and cumulative. Further, they contend that lower achieving students are the most likely to benefit from increases in teacher effectiveness. Taken together, these multiple sources of evidence—however different in nature—all conclude that quality teachers are a critical determinant of student achievement. In the current policy climate of standards-based reform, these findings make a strong case for gaining a better understanding of what really accounts for these effects. In other words, what is teacher quality?

The resource-intensive nature of teachers coupled with the empirical evidence documenting the critical role of teacher quality in realizing student achievement implies that teacher policy is a promising avenue toward better realizing goals of efficiency, equity, and adequacy in public education. Indeed, recommendations for reforming the preparation of teachers have become commonplace in reports aimed at improving public education (Bush 1987). For instance, almost two decades ago in its call for improved teacher preparation, the National Commission on Excellence in Education (1983) stated that "teacher preparation programs are too heavily weighted with courses in educational methods at the expense of courses in subjects to be taught." The Carnegie Foundation for the Advancement of Teaching recommended that teacher education programs require a 3.0 grade point average for admission, and that teachers complete courses in an academic-core subject in four years before spending a fifth year learning about education (Boyer 1983). Likewise, the Holmes Group (1986) advised that all major universities with substantial enrollments of preservice teachers (i.e., those who are preparing to enter the teaching profession but who are not yet classroom teachers) should adopt the four-year liberal arts baccalaureate as a prerequisite for acceptance into their teacher education programs. A decade later the National Commission on Teaching and America's Future proposed major changes in teacher preparation and licensure, recommending that authority over these matters be shifted from public officials to professional organizations (NCTAF 1996).[4]

The recent federal education legislation, *No Child Left Behind* (NCLB), further underlines the importance of having a high-quality teacher in every classroom in every school. The Bush Administration's proposal, which specifies what defines a "highly qualified" teacher, is based on the premise that teacher excellence is vital to realizing improved student achievement.[5] This legislation, along with typical hiring and compensation systems, assumes that years of teaching experience, teacher certification, engagement in certain types of coursework, and performance on standardized assessments are indicators of high-quality teachers.[6]

The purpose of this analysis is to review existing empirical evidence to draw conclusions about the specific characteristics that are linked with teacher performance. Greater clarity on the empirical evidence regarding teacher quality can inform the wisdom of current practice, guide state efforts in the struggle with NCLB compliance regarding teachers, and provide direction for future teacher policy.

The research context

In the context of this intense activity surrounding teacher policy, it makes sense to turn to the existing evidence on which teacher attributes are related to teacher effectiveness in order to guide policy decisions about hiring, compensation, and distribution with respect to teachers. However, the literature on teacher quality and qualifications has typically been viewed as inconsistent and inconclusive. Much of this perception has been fueled by a set of analyses conducted by Eric Hanushek over the past two decades. In his meta-analysis of studies examining the impact of several key educational resources on student achievement, Hanushek (1981, 1986, 1996, 1997) concluded that there is no systematic relationship between educational inputs and student performance. For example, with respect to teacher characteristics, Hanushek (1997) identified 171 estimates related to the impact of "teacher education" on student performance. Of these, he reported that 9% were statistically significant and positive, 5% were statistically significant and negative, and 86% were statistically insignificant. In addition, Hanushek included 41 estimates of the impact of teacher test scores on student outcomes. Of these, 37% were statistically significant and positive, 10% were statistically significant and negative, and 54% were not statistically significant. Finally, of the 207 studies that estimate the effect of teacher experience, 29% of the estimates were statistically significant and positive, 5% were statistically significant and negative, and 66% were not statistically significant.

Hanushek's conclusions that resources are not systematically related to outcomes has been hotly challenged by a number of other researchers with respect to his "vote-counting" methodology (Hedges, Laine, and Greenwald 1994a, 1994b; Greenwald, Hedges, and Laine 1996; Krueger 2002) and how he weighted (or didn't weight) the studies (Krueger 2002). The work by Hedges, Laine, and Greenwald demonstrated that the use of more sophisticated meta-analytical techniques to analyze the same set of studies included in Hanushek's review produced far more consistent and compelling findings regarding the effect of educational resources—including variables related to the quality and quantity of teachers—on student achievement. Krueger's (2002) critique of Hanushek's methodology centered on how the various studies were weighted in Hanushek's analysis. Essentially, Hanushek labeled each estimate of an effect as a "study," so that one article could have several estimates, or studies, that are factored into Hanushek's count of positive, negative, or statistically insignificant (positive and negative) effects. Krueger argues that this approach weights the various studies by the number of different estimates of the effect of a particular variable they include. Further, he contends that studies that report negative or statistically insignificant findings are more likely to include more estimates than those that find statistically significant positive effects. Krueger's re-analysis of the studies that Hanushek included on the effect of pupil-teacher ratio and the effect of per-pupil expenditures demonstrates that other approaches to weighting the studies lead to a more consistent and positive story about the effect of these resources on student achievement.

In addition to these criticisms, Hanushek's analysis was limited to the education production function literature, i.e., studies examining how educational resources (inputs) are systematically transformed into educational outcomes (outputs). On one hand, this set of studies could be argued to be too inclusive in the sense that even those studies that simply included an educational resource as a control variable might be inappropriately considered (e.g., a study including both class size and per-pupil expenditures). On the other hand, the production function literature could be contested as too exclusive in the sense that other methodological approaches, particularly those that allow the researcher to focus on more refined measures of what teachers know and can do, can also make valuable contributions to what we know about the value of educational resources. In contrast to the work of Hanushek and others who have looked at specific subgroups of studies (see, for example, Mayer, Mullens, Moore, and Ralph 2000; Wayne and Youngs 2003; Whitehurst 2002), the literature review presented here represents an analysis of a wide variety of empirical studies examining the impact of teacher attributes on teacher performance.

The approach taken here is similar to that used by Wilson, Floden, and Ferrini-Mundy (2001) in their review of the research on teacher preparation conducted for the U.S. Department of Education. Empirical studies that conform to a variety of accepted methodological approaches and use a range of measures of teacher effectiveness are used to ascertain what existing evidence says about the relationship between teacher attributes and their performance. In addition, this approach pays close attention to a number of contextual factors (e.g., level of education, subject area, type of student) as a way of drawing conclusions across studies. Clearly, the context of teaching is important and may affect the impact of the teacher attributes considered in this analysis. In fact, when existing studies are considered as a whole (without breaking them down by contextual factors such as subject area or grade level), findings tend to be inconsistent across studies; context variables may help to explain the apparent inconsistency of the existing research. In other words, a particular teacher attribute (e.g., a subject-specific master's degree) may be an important predictor of teacher effectiveness in some contexts (e.g., high school math), but may not matter at all or may even have a negative effect in other contexts (e.g., first-grade reading). This careful attention to the context of teaching, wherever possible, helps to tease out some effects that would otherwise go undetected in reviews that neglect to consider these factors. The goal of this study is to sort through the available evidence to draw conclusions about what matters, what has been studied but has not been shown to matter, and what has not been adequately studied.

In the face of such seemingly inconsistent and inconclusive evidence, policy makers are side-stepping the research (or relying only on those studies that support their positions) to move forward with teacher policies, often without the benefit of research to guide their efforts. However, research can, and should, play a role in these decisions. For instance, numerous measures of what a teacher knows and can do have been routinely assumed to be important (at least as indicated through hiring strategies, salary schedules, and teacher reform agendas). However, questions continue to persist about what exactly a quality teacher is. In other words, what teacher characteristics have been found to predict teacher effectiveness? This is a fundamental question that must precede policy discussions concerning what kinds of teacher qualities and qualifications to promote in aspiring teachers, whom to recruit and hire, what factors to use in setting salary schedules, and how to distribute teachers across different types of schools and classrooms to achieve equity and adequacy goals. This analysis examines the existing empirical literature on the relationship between teacher attributes and their effectiveness with the goal of informing policy on investing in teacher quality.

The next chapter describes the methodology used to review the literature on the relationship between teacher characteristics and their performance, and the chapter that follows presents the findings from this literature review. The final chapter concludes with a discussion of the implications of these findings for future research and policy.

CHAPTER 2

Methodology and framework

The literature on teacher quality and qualifications is vast and varied. This book focuses on empirical studies that represent a variety of methodological approaches, measures of teacher effectiveness, and specific teacher characteristics. Given that teacher quality is multifaceted, this review creates a framework of five broad categories of teacher attributes generally reflected in teacher compensation systems and typically assumed to be indicative of teacher quality: (1) experience, (2) preparation programs and degrees, (3) type of certification, (4) coursework taken in preparation for the profession, and (5) teachers' own test scores.

All studies included in this review are empirical and designed to explicitly measure the relationship between teacher characteristics and elements of teacher performance. These studies, conducted across the past three decades, are primarily drawn from peer-reviewed journals and focus on education in the United States.

This literature review used a variety of methods to identify studies examining the relationship between teacher attributes and teacher effectiveness. Searches of several electronic databases identified a wide range of documents that were reviewed for inclusion. These searches included using keywords regarding teacher quality and qualifications to search ERIC, PsychLit, EconLit, Social Sciences Citation Index, and Science Citation Index. Additional studies were found by reviewing reference lists from published articles, books, book chapters, and reports dealing with teacher quality and qualifications. Key journals that routinely publish research on teachers, teacher policy, and teacher effectiveness were also used as a source for locating relevant literature.

Several criteria guided the selection of studies included in this review. First, the studies had to be empirical rather than theoretical or conceptual treatments of the impact of teacher attributes on effectiveness. Second, all studies included in this review were designed explicitly to examine the relationship between policy-relevant teacher characteristics and measures of teacher performance.[7] Third, the studies included in this review were primarily drawn from academic journals that engage in formal peer-review processes as one quality-control consideration.[8] In addition, a number of highly influential and widely cited books and chapters are included that provide empirical evidence on the relationship between teacher attributes and teacher performance. Fourth, the studies are from the past three decades. Finally, all studies included in the review focus on education in the United States. The goal of the review was not to "boil down" the studies to quantitative summaries of what matters, but rather to synthesize the literature in a way that brings qualitative meaning to the array of studies that have been conducted.

The studies included in this review vary along a number of dimensions. First, while all of the studies assess the relationship between teacher characteristics and teacher performance, the specific outcomes vary across studies. Perhaps the most straightforward measure of teacher performance is the achievement gains realized by their students on standardized tests. A recent review by Wayne and Youngs (2003) identified only 21 studies that empirically examined the impact of teacher characteristics on U.S. student achievement while adequately controlling for prior achievement test scores and socioeconomic status. In addition, many other studies have explored the relationship between teacher attributes and their performance in terms of principals' evaluations of teachers, measures of teacher competence and skills, grade point averages of students, and teachers' perceptions of their own performance and the quality and impact of their preparation. In an effort to cast the widest net possible in understanding the effect of teacher attributes, this review includes studies that measure teacher performance in all of these ways. This broad approach is particularly important because some educational goals may not be adequately captured by student performance as measured by standardized achievement tests.

Second, the studies vary in terms of the methodology used. Some rely on sophisticated multivariate psychometric or econometric techniques using large national datasets to test hypothesized models that include measures of teacher quality to predict educational outcomes (usually student achievement) while controlling for other factors. Others use matched-comparison designs to examine how the effectiveness of teachers with certain professional qualifications differs from that of teachers without those qualifications, controlling for the characteristics on which teachers were matched. Still others use interview and observational data to examine the experiences of relatively small samples of teachers and teacher candidates with the goal of gaining insight about the contribution of these experiences to teacher effectiveness. While the U.S. Department of Education is currently placing heavy emphasis on "scientifically based research" (see Whitehurst 2002), the tradition of research in teacher education has long relied on a wide array of empirical approaches and methodological strategies (Kennedy 1996, 1999). In an effort to examine the full range of empirical evidence, a variety of studies are included along this "methodological continuum," as well as findings from other literature reviews on the subject of teacher quality. This presentation of the studies describes the basic tenets of each method used (e.g., sample size, type of analysis).

Finally, the studies included in this review vary in terms of the specific teacher attributes they examine. Teacher quality is multifaceted, including factors related to the quantity and the quality of preservice education, certification status (regular, provisional, emergency, not certified), highest academic degree earned, teachers' own test scores, years of experience, and so forth. These different measures all presumably contribute to a teacher's capacity to effectively educate children. This review focuses on a set of policy-relevant characteristics often assumed to be reflective of teacher quality, at least as evident in hiring practices, salary schedules, and other teacher policies by exploring the degree to which certain qualifications (e.g., certification status, degree level, years of experience) have been empirically shown to be indicators of teacher quality. In doing so, this review sheds light on a number of key policy questions. For example, are *qualified* teachers, as judged by various teacher attributes, likely to be *quality* teachers? Likewise, are hiring and compensation policies that reward certain qualifications equivalent to investments in teacher quality? Does the *No Child Left Behind* legislation that requires "highly qualified teachers" really hold promise for enhancing the quality of teachers, particularly in Title I schools and classrooms that serve high concentrations of disadvantaged students? Scrutinizing the qualifications generally assumed to be indicators of teacher quality is a critical exercise if we are serious about the goals of efficiency, equity, and adequacy in public education.

A framework of five broad categories is used to organize the teacher characteristics assumed to reflect teacher quality.

1) Teacher experience is a common component of teacher salary schedules. Typically measured in terms of the number of years of service as a teacher, experience is a measure of teacher quality to the degree that more experienced teachers have amassed more knowledge and better skills through on-the-job learning.

2) Teacher preparation programs and degrees include formal preservice preparation programs as well as degrees earned. This set of indicators includes graduation from an education program, the quality of the institution attended, participation in an extended teacher education program, and acquisition of an advanced degree. These measures of teacher quality tend to be rather crude indicators of what teachers know and can do because they do not account for the actual material covered or the quality of the experience.[9]

3) Teacher certification indicates whether teachers have fulfilled the requirements for state licensure. The specific requirements for certification vary from state to state, but typically include completion of an accredited teacher education program, student-teaching experience, and a formal recommendation from the institution of higher education. Many states also require that teachers pass a certification test. There are several classifications of certification including regular or standard certification, provisional certification, advanced certification, alternative certification, and private school certification.

4) The specific coursework taken by teachers in preparation for the profession is the fourth measure of teacher quality. This indicator provides information about both the amount (e.g., number of courses, number of credits) and the type (e.g., pedagogical, content-specific, field experiences) of courses taken.

5) Teachers' own test scores are the final set of indicators of teacher quality. The different assessments included in the literature are varied, but they all indicate some aspect of teacher knowledge, proficiency, and/or level of literacy.

Based on this review of the research, several broad conclusions can be drawn about the relationship between these teacher attributes and teacher performance. These conclusions provide a relatively comprehensive understanding about what characteristics really count as teacher quality, at least as indicated by the broad set of empirical studies reviewed here.

Several caveats are worth noting. First, given the inclusive nature of this literature review, the studies included are variable in quality. While the criterion that studies be published in peer-reviewed journals reflects an effort to control for this variability, unevenness in quality across studies remains. This review describes study designs, including sample sizes and methodological approaches used. In drawing conclusions about causal links between teacher attributes and teacher effectiveness, only those studies that are designed to isolate these sorts of effects are considered. In other words, individual studies contribute to the conclusions only what their designs allow.

Second, while the review is intended to be quite inclusive in nature, drawing on a wide array of studies that represent various methodological approaches, consider multiple measures of teacher performance, and use a variety of teacher characteristics, the analysis is limited to *measurable* teacher attributes assumed to reflect teacher quality. It is important to recognize that many characteristics of good teachers are difficult to measure (e.g., leadership styles, sensitivity to students, respect for diversity), but should not be ignored in discussions of teacher quality. For example, some efforts have been made to evaluate and even compensate teachers based on a formal system of teacher observation by qualified trained observers (see Odden and Kelley (2002) for examples and a discussion of this approach). While the costs of this approach to measuring teacher quality may be quite high, teacher observation could provide a way to get beyond the more conventional indicators of teacher quality that have traditionally served as the basis for teacher hiring and compensation. Nonetheless, this review focuses on measurable teacher characteristics that are typically assumed to indicate teacher quality, are common qualifications that serve as a basis for teacher hiring and compensation decisions, and are often the object of teacher policy designed to improve the efficiency, equity, and adequacy of the public education system.[10]

Third, as described earlier, this review includes five categories of teacher characteristics. While a concerted effort is made here to narrow the definitions of teacher attributes to distinguishable policy-relevant characteristics, there remains a great deal of variability in what these measures truly mean. For instance, certification means different things in different places. Likewise, not all pedagogical courses contain similar content or are of equal quality. This review makes an effort to disaggregate the studies to make sense of the evidence on the impact of specific teacher qualities and qualifications. However, the unique context and purpose of each study limit the generalizability of the findings.

CHAPTER 3

What the evidence says about the effect of teacher attributes on teacher performance

The best available current evidence indicates that teacher quality does matter. Investments in teachers with experience, certain preparation and credentials, specific pedagogic and content coursework, and test scores can yield improvements in student performance. Evidence of these effects varies by level of schooling (elementary and high school), types of students (advantaged and disadvantaged), and subject areas (mathematics, science, and English). The review is organized around the five categories of teacher attributes: teacher experience, teacher preparation programs and degrees, type of teacher certification, coursework taken by teachers in preparation for the profession, and teachers' own test scores. Specific findings are summarized at the beginning of each section.

Numerous studies have examined the relationship between various teacher attributes and teacher performance. These studies reflect much variability in terms of the teacher characteristics examined, the educational outcome of interest, the methodology employed, and the findings reported. The purpose of this analysis is to make sense of this seemingly unwieldy body of literature focused on the relationship between teacher characteristics and teacher effectiveness. More specifically, this chapter explores what has been identified about the impact of multiple measures of what a teacher knows and can do (particularly those qualifications that are assumed in hiring and compensation policies to reflect "quality") on teacher performance. The five sections that follow present the findings organized by category of teacher attributes. The final section arrays the findings of this diverse body of research into a discrete set of lessons that can inform policy makers concerned with the preparation and distribution of teachers across classrooms.

The five categories of teacher quality indicators are arranged beginning with the crudest measure of teacher quality and concluding with measures that are arguably more indicative of what teachers know and can do.

Teacher experience[11]

A set of quasi-experimental studies designed to test the causal relationship between teacher experience and student achievement reveals a positive relationship between these two variables. At the elementary level, this relationship is most evident during the first several years of teaching. Student performance increases with each year of teacher experience during the first few years of teaching but drops off after that. There is also some evidence that positive effects reemerge among very experienced teachers (those with more than 14 years of teaching experience). Estimates of the effect of teacher experience on high school student achievement suggest that experience has a more sustained effect, continuing later into teachers' careers.

To the extent that on-the-job learning occurs and leads to better teaching practices, experience can be construed as a measure of teacher quality. Some have argued that this notion of "learning by doing" has the most pronounced effect on teacher effectiveness in the initial years of teaching (Murnane and Phillips 1981). Teacher experience is an interesting variable from a policy perspective. First and foremost, experience is a central component of most teacher salary schedules (Odden and Kelly 2002). In addition, to the degree that teacher experience is an important predictor of student performance, policy efforts should be made to distribute teacher experience more equitably across schools and districts. Experience typically affords teachers more opportunity to choose the schools and districts where they want to work, and more experienced teachers often choose the best, most advantaged schools. Further, the relatively high turnover rates in low-income, low-achieving schools result in even lower levels of experience in these environments (Allgood and Rice 2002). These distributional issues give rise to questions about the degree to which experience is an important dimension of teacher effectiveness and whether policies should aim to more equitably distribute experienced teachers.

Many studies have included teacher experience as an independent variable predicting student achievement or some other measure of teacher performance. In fact, Hanushek (1997) identified 207 such studies, more than any other teacher characteristic, in his review of the education production function literature. As described in Chapter 1, Hanushek found that 29% of the estimates of the impact of experience on teacher quality were statistically significant and positive, 5% were statistically significant and negative, and 66% were not statistically significant. While the majority of these studies report statistically insignificant effects, it is worth noting that, of the statistically significant findings, positive effects are reported almost six times as often as negative effects. As for the preponderance of statistically insignificant effects, it is not clear from Hanushek's analysis whether the studies were actually designed to test the impact of experience on student achievement, what other variables were included in the models tested, or what measure of teacher experience was employed by the studies. Further casting doubt on Hanushek's conclusions about teacher experience, Greenwald, Hedges, and Laine (1996) conducted a more sophisticated meta-analysis of education production function literature from which they concluded that teacher experience is, in fact, related to achievement.

One explanation for the discordant evidence about the inconsistent impact of teacher experience relates to the measurement of this variable. Most schools districts measure and reward teacher experience in terms of the years worked in the district. However, studies examining the impact of teacher experience could instead measure this variable as the total number of years that the teacher has taught. In other words, teacher effectiveness should be estimated as a function of all the years of experience, not just the years taught in a particular district. Because most studies do not indicate whether teacher experience is measured as the total number of years teaching or the number of years teaching in a particular school district, it is not clear the degree to which this problem clouds the data.

Another explanation for the inconsistent evidence on teacher experience is the way this variable has been used in studies. Many analyses have included teacher experience as a control variable in models testing the effect of other variables on student achievement. Typically these studies enter experience as a single, continuous variable and find no evidence of a linear relationship between teacher experience and their effectiveness. On the other hand, studies that focus on teacher experience as the key independent variable (i.e., the treatment) have found that nonlinear models are far more likely to capture an effect for this variable. Consequently, this review considers only those studies that explicitly measure teacher experience as a key treatment; these analyses are designed to ascertain the nonlinear effect of experience on teacher effectiveness.

In his 1975 book, *The Impact of School Resources on the Learning of Inner-City Children*, Murnane was among the first to find a relationship between teacher experience and student achievement. His quasi-experimental study of the impact of resources on 875 inner-city black elementary school children found that, controlling for other factors, teacher effectiveness dramatically increases over the first three years of teaching, peaking in the third to fifth year. He was unable to detect an effect for experience after five years.

In a later study, Murnane and Phillips (1981) examined a sample of black elementary school students from predominately low-income families in one city. The sample included 205 third-grade students, 207 fourth-grade students, 199 fifth-grade students, and 203 sixth-grade students. School records provided information on student achievement test scores, class assignments, and school characteristics. Student background information was collected through interviews with parents, and information on teacher background, attitude, and behavior was collected through a survey. The researchers were interested in estimating the impact of teacher classroom behavior and teacher characteristics on student vocabulary achievement. Number of years of experience was one of the teacher background variables of interest in this study. Controlling for a variety of student and teacher background variables, Murnane and Phillips found that, among teachers in their first seven years of teaching, experience has a significant positive effect on elementary school student achievement. The researchers found a weak negative relationship between experience and student achievement among teachers with eight to 14 years of experience, and a positive effect of experience on student achievement for teachers with 15 or more years of teaching experience. They argue that the early-career effect is likely to reflect "learning by doing," while the later-career effect is a "vintage effect" that reflects differences in the average abilities of teachers who entered the profession at various points in time.

Ferguson (1991) found that teacher experience accounted for slightly more than 10% of the variation in student reading and math scores across almost 900 Texas school districts serving over 2.4 million students. Ferguson utilized two teacher experience variables: the percentage of teachers in a district with five to nine years of experience and the percentage of teachers in a district with nine or more years of experience. In the elementary grades, Ferguson found that these two teacher experience variables had roughly equal coefficients, suggesting that once teachers have five years' experience, additional years of teaching do not add to their effectiveness. For high school students, however, Ferguson found that teachers with nine or more years of experience were associated with higher student scores than teachers with only five to nine years of experience.

Ferguson and Ladd's (1996) analysis of statewide Alabama data investigated the effect of teachers with five or more years of experience on student achievement at the district level. Their sample included 29,544 students in third, fourth, eighth, and ninth grades. Controlling for a variety of school and student variables, they found that teacher experience of five years of more exerts no statistically significant effect on math or reading achievement.

Grissmer et al.'s (2000) analysis of state-level National Assessment of Educational Progress (NAEP) data included an investigation of the relationship between the proportion of teachers in a state with more than two years of experience and elementary student performance on the NAEP. They found that in states where a high proportion of teachers have at least two years of experience, there is a discernible, positive effect on achievement; however, the researchers found no evidence that additional years of teacher experience influence student achievement. Grissmer et al. interpret this as a "turnover effect" because high teacher turnover usually results in more teachers with fewer years of experience. The researchers found that a portion of interstate variation in NAEP scores between students with similar family characteristics can be traced to teacher turnover rates; thus, in states with lower rates of teacher turnover, NAEP scores are higher.

Summary of findings on teacher experience
While research indicates that there is a relationship between student achievement and teacher experience, at the elementary level of education it appears that the relationship is most evident in the first several years of teaching, with some evidence of vintage effects for very experienced teachers. Estimates of the effect of teacher experience on high school student achievement suggest that experience has a more sustained effect that continues later into teachers' careers.

Teacher preparation programs and degrees

*Primarily qualitative in nature, the studies on **teacher education programs** reveal mixed evidence regarding the degree to which these programs contribute to teachers' knowledge. Several studies identify specific components of teacher education programs that are most important (e.g., subject-specific pedagogy, classroom management). These studies offer limited evidence regarding the contribution of teacher education programs to teacher competencies or student achievement.*

*In terms of the **selectivity of the programs** (i.e., the quality of the institution) attended by teachers, the evidence suggests a modest positive effect of institutional selectivity on student performance at the elementary level and a positive effect at the high school level. Evidence also suggests that, at the elementary level, the positive effect of teacher quality, as indicated by the selectivity of the institution they attended, may be more pronounced for low-income students.*

*Studies of **extended teacher education programs** suggest positive effects on entry into the profession and retention rates, but no clear effect on teacher performance, at least as indicated by principal evaluations. Additionally, a number of quasi-experimental studies on whether **advanced degrees** contribute to teacher quality have been conducted. These studies have a history of showing that a teacher's advanced degrees have no effect on student achievement, and sometimes even have negative effects for elementary student achievement. However, a recent wave of studies that take into consideration the subject area of the advanced degree and the teaching assignment have found a positive effect of subject-specific advanced degrees on student achievement. These studies are limited to high school mathematics and, to a lesser extent, science. In one study, this effect was limited to black students.*

One indicator of teacher quality concerns the "package" of professional preparation, without explicit attention to the individual components of that package (e.g., specific courses) or to the skills and knowledge acquired. Teacher preparation is one of the most popular aspects of teacher quality among policy makers because these qualifications are typically a key component of state licensure, which serves as the gatekeeper for the profession, and because of their broad applicability. There is considerable debate in the policy arena about the appropriate requirements for teacher preparation, the role of traditional teacher education programs, and the level of degree teachers should hold.

The broad issue of teacher preparation programs and credentials has been studied in terms of whether teachers graduated from a teacher education program (including the quality of the institution attended), and whether they completed an extended teacher education program or earned an advanced degree. Each of these components of teacher preparation is discussed below.

Teacher education programs

Several studies have explored the impact of knowledge gained in teacher education programs on subsequent on-the-job performance. Based on questionnaire responses from 1,851 principals and 770 teachers across grade levels, Pigge (1978) reported that teachers perceived that the competencies most necessary to their work were those learned on the job. In contrast, a modest negative correlation characterized the relationship between the competencies teachers thought they needed and those developed through their teacher education programs.

Clark, Smith, Newby, and Cook (1985) used observational interview and survey data from 44 first-year teachers and 27 student teachers from a number of different teacher education programs to study the impact of teacher education programs as a source of ideas for subsequent teaching practices. The sample included 32 elementary and 12 secondary teachers. The researchers found that the most frequently perceived origin of ideas for teaching practices were teachers' "own ideas." The second most common sources of teaching innovations were student teaching experiences and content from teacher education courses. Taken together, the teacher education program accounted for about one-third of the practices used by the teachers. It is important to note, however, that a good education course would presumably be one that prepares students to develop their "own ideas" when they become teachers (i.e., to problem solve on the job), so this study may underestimate the effect of teacher education programs. Findings from the studies by Pigge (1978) and Clark, Smith, Newby, and Cook (1985) highlight the importance of the student teacher field experiences component of teacher education programs.

Adams and Krockover (1997) conducted an interpretive study of four beginning high school science teachers who completed a teacher preparation program at a large midwestern university. The researchers used interviews, observations, videotapes of classroom events, and document analysis to gain insight into the contribution of the teacher education program to various aspects of the teachers' professional knowledge. The teachers identified the teacher education program as the source of their knowledge of student-centered instruction, general pedagogical knowledge (including classroom routines and discipline), and pedagogical content knowledge (including instructional strategies). Although the researchers found variation in what the four teachers learned from the teacher preparation courses, the teacher education program was found to provide these novice teachers with a framework by which to organize, understand, and reflect on their experiences in the classroom.

Several studies identified particular components of teacher education programs as important, with noteworthy agreement about the subject-specific pedagogical training that teachers receive. Hollingsworth (1989) describes the findings from the initial year of a longitudinal study designed to investigate changes in preservice teachers' knowledge and beliefs about reading instruction before, during, and after a fifth-year teacher education program. The study participants included 14 preservice teachers, 32 cooperating teachers, six university supervisors, and two reading course instructors. Data included interviews with and observations of teachers as they entered the teacher education program, attended reading classes, and taught reading in school classrooms. Hollingsworth concludes that some teacher education factors were more effective than others in preparing the preservice teachers in this study to manage classrooms, teach reading, and understand student learning. Specifically, the study identifies the importance of understanding preservice teachers' prior beliefs to inform university course design, the value of cognitive dissonance in practice teaching contexts, the need to make classroom-management knowledge routine before attending to subject-specific pedagogy, and the importance of a strong academic foundation to the teaching knowledge base.

Grossman (1989) approaches the question from a different perspective by studying three teachers who entered the teaching profession without teacher education. All three teachers in the study were well prepared in English, their subject area. Data for these case studies included classroom observations and five in-depth, structured interviews with each teacher. Grossman concludes that "without formal systems of induction into teaching, learning to teach is left largely to chance....While subject-matter knowledge, good character, and the inclination to teach are important characteristics of beginning teachers, they do not necessarily lead to a pedagogical understanding of subject matter nor to a theoretical understanding of how students learn a particular subject" (p. 207). This study argues for the important role of teacher education programs in preparing teachers to apply their subject-matter knowledge to classroom instruction.

Grossman et al. (2003) conducted a longitudinal study that followed 10 teachers from their last year of preservice training through their first two years of teaching. The sample consisted of five elementary school teachers, two middle school teachers, and three high school teachers. A variety of data sources were used including interviews with teachers, classroom observation, and principal input. The researchers found that teacher education provided the teachers with a conceptual framework for thinking about and teaching writing. The teacher education program provided the new teachers with a range of instructional strategies; moreover, the teachers in the study attributed their ability to be reflective about their teaching to the teacher education program.

Several studies examined the effect of teacher education programs on teacher competencies or student achievement. Dewalt and Ball (1987) relied on classroom observations to study the relationship between teacher training and 12 dimensions of competence: (1) academic learning time, (2) accountability, (3) clarity of structure, (4) individual differences, (5) evaluation, (6) affective climate, (7) learner self-concept, (8) meaningfulness, (9) planning, (10) questioning skill, (11) reinforcement, and (12) close supervision. The sample included 230 beginning secondary school teachers, 57 of whom had not acquired the credentials to qualify them as fully prepared to teach and 173 who had full preparation. The group of fully prepared teachers comprised higher percentages of male and white teachers than the group of those not fully prepared. All subject areas were represented in the sample. The researchers found that unprepared teachers scored higher than prepared teachers on two competencies: accountability (the idea that competent teachers know the importance of holding learners responsible for completing assigned tasks) and questioning skills (the notion that competent teachers know how to phrase convergent, divergent, and probing questions and to use them to develop learners' academic knowledge). No other differences between the two groups were found. The researchers conclude that their analysis does not support the belief that teacher training increases teacher competence along the 12 dimensions measured in this study. They did find less variance in the mean teacher scores on the 12 competencies for prepared teachers, suggesting that teacher training may standardize the competence of beginning teachers. The Dewalt and Ball study only examined the effect of teacher education programs on these 12 competencies and did not link these competencies to student achievement or teacher effectiveness.

In a case study of a single high school mathematics teacher who taught before and after formal teacher preparation, Valli and Agostinelli (1993) provide insights about the contributions of the teacher education program in this single case. The study is based on data from interviews, observations, and reflections by the teacher. Before formal preparation, the teacher reported weaknesses in controlling the class and maintaining order; after preparation she found herself more capable of respectfully controlling classroom interactions with and among students, and keeping the students on task. In terms of instruction, after preparation the teacher was more organized with lesson plans; was more student-oriented rather than teacher-oriented; was able to ask more probing, open-ended questions; and offered a wider range of assignments. While many of these changes may be the result of a variety of factors, including more teaching experience and the knowledge and confidence that comes with that experience, the teacher attributed these changes to the coursework and experiences that were part of the teacher preparation program.

Only one study of the impact of participation in a teacher education program on teacher quality used a quasi-experimental design to control for other factors. Murnane (1975) studied the relationship between teacher characteristics and teacher performance in terms of student achievement in reading and mathematics. His sample included two cohorts of urban elementary school students in the second and third grades. More than 400 students were included in each cohort. He found that in one cohort, third-grade students assigned to teachers who had majored in education realized a higher mathematics achievement gain relative to their counterparts assigned to teachers who did not major in education. This effect was not apparent for third graders in the other cohort, for third graders' reading achievement gain, or for the achievement gains of the second graders in either cohort in mathematics or reading.

Selectivity of teacher preparation programs

Arguably, better teacher education programs yield more positive outcomes in terms of teacher performance. Several multivariate studies controlled for student and teacher characteristics to estimate the effect of the selectivity of the institution attended by teacher candidates. Summers and Wolfe (1975) analyzed a random sample of 627 sixth-grade students, 553 eighth-grade students, and 716 twelfth-grade students from an urban school district to estimate the impact of a number of education inputs on student achievement. Controlling for a variety of other factors, the researchers found that the Gourman rating (which measures college selectivity) of the college the teacher attended is related to teacher effectiveness. Students assigned to teachers who attended higher-rated colleges tended to score higher than their counterparts whose teachers were educated at lower-rated institutions. This effect was apparent at the elementary level and was most pronounced for low-income students, even when other teacher attributes were entered in the models.

In their study of several hundred black, predominately low-income elementary school students in one city, Murnane and Phillips (1981) included a variable indicating that the teacher attended a prestigious college in their model predicting student achievement. No information was provided on the system used to rate colleges in this study. Controlling for a variety of student and teacher background factors, the researchers found no evidence of a relationship between institutional prestige and students' Iowa Test of Basic Skills vocabulary gain scores (i.e., how much scores improved) for grades three, four, five, or six.

Finally, in their analysis of the nationally representative[12] High School & Beyond data,[13] Ehrenberg and Brewer (1994) coded the selectivity of institutions attended by teachers using Barron's six-category rating system of the admissions selectivity of the school in that year. The researchers found that, holding other factors constant, the average selectivity of the undergraduate institutions attend by teachers has a positive effect on student gain scores. Disaggregating by race and ethnicity, the positive effect was apparent for white and black students, but was not statistically significant for Hispanic students.

Extended teacher preparation programs and advanced degrees

Recent teacher policy trends have emphasized post-baccalaureate training programs for teachers, including professional, education specialist, and master's degrees (Turner 1998). These programs generally add to the number of years of formal education and often involve acquiring an additional academic degree.

Andrew and Schwab (1995) studied 1,390 education school graduates from 11 institutions to draw conclusions about four-year programs versus extended teacher education programs with respect to four outcomes: entry of teachers into the profession, retention in the profession, classroom performance, and leadership behavior. The analysis was based on self-reported data from teachers and on principals' performance evaluations. The researchers found that graduates of extended programs entered the teaching profession at significantly higher rates and showed higher rates of retention than their counterparts from the four-year programs. Some evidence was found to suggest that four-year teachers were more likely than extended-program graduates to gradually replace all or some of their teaching responsibilities with administrative or non-teaching leadership roles. No statistically significant differences were found between four-year and extended-program graduates in terms of their performance in the classroom.

In his investigation of extended formal teacher preparation, Andrew (1990) compared graduates from four- and five-year teacher education programs at the same institution. The four-year program had lower standards for entry, less emphasis on subject-specific coursework, and a more limited supervised student-teaching experience. The samples used for the study were randomly selected from individuals who had graduated from the two programs during the 10-year period between 1976 and 1986. The final sample included 144 graduates of the five-year program and 163 graduates of the four-year program, all of whom completed surveys administered as part of the study. Comparisons of the two groups reveal that more graduates of the five-year program entered and remained in the teaching profession than graduates of the four-year program. Further, graduates of the five-year program had a more positive perception of their education program and were more satisfied with their careers.

A number of studies have also examined the impact of earning an advanced degree on teacher effectiveness. In fact, degree level attained by the teacher has been a common variable in quantitative regression-based studies examining teacher characteristics that contribute to student achievement. The majority of these studies found no statistically significant effect of teacher degree level on teacher performance as measured by student achievement gains, controlling for student background and other teacher and school characteristics. Summers and Wolfe's (1977) analysis of urban education concluded that, controlling for other factors, teacher degree beyond a bachelor's has no discernible effect on teacher performance as measured by student achievement in the sixth, eighth, and twelfth grades. Based their analysis of 500 fourth-grade students in one urban school district, Link and Ratledge (1979) found no statistically significant effect of teachers' advanced degrees on student achievement, controlling for other factors. Murnane and Phillips' (1981) analysis of urban elementary education found no statistically significant effect of master's degrees on student achievement in grades three through six. Harnish's (1987) analysis of the nationally representative High School & Beyond data also revealed no statistically significant effect of teacher degree level on student performance. Ehrenberg and Brewer (1994) used the same High School & Beyond data to estimate the impact of school and teacher characteristics on the achievement of students from different backgrounds. They found evidence of a statistically significant relationship between a teacher's possession of a master's degree and student achievement, but only for black students. Monk's (1994) analysis of data from the Longitudinal Study of American Youth (LSAY) data,[14] a nationally representative dataset of middle and high school education, also found little convincing evidence of a relationship between teacher degree and student achievement in mathematics or science at the secondary level.

In addition, several studies of elementary education report a negative relationship between teacher degree and teacher performance, as measured by student achievement, controlling for student background and other teacher characteristics. In his analysis of urban elementary education, Murnane (1975) found some evidence that teachers with master's degrees actually have a negative impact on the mathematics achievement of second and third graders, while a teacher's degree level had no statistically significant effect on reading achievement. Eberts and Stone's (1984) study of public schools found a negative relationship between teacher degree level and the mathematics achievement gains of fourth-grade students. That is, teachers with higher degrees in mathematics were found to result in lower student test scores. Kiesling's (1984) study of the impact of instructional time on students' reading performance relied on a sample of 3,374 elementary students in New York City. This analysis also revealed some evidence of a negative relationship between teacher degree level and student performance.

More recently, Rowan, Correnti, and Miller (2002) used survey data from *Prospects: The Congressionally Mandated Study of Educational Opportunity* to study the effect of teachers on elementary student achievement in mathematics and reading. They used hierarchical growth models that controlled for a variety of home and social background factors to test the effect of teacher attributes on mathematics and reading achievement for two cohorts of students: students in grades one through three and students in grades three through six. They found that students assigned to teachers holding a bachelor's or a master's degree in English performed no differently than those assigned to teachers without the subject-specific degree. Students who were taught by a teacher with a degree in mathematics actually did worse than those who were taught by teachers not holding a mathematics degree.[15]

Finally, several recent studies report a positive relationship between advanced degrees and teacher effectiveness as measured by student performance. Ferguson and Ladd's (1996) econometric analysis of 29,544 Alabama students found that the percentage of teachers in a school holding a master's degree has a positive effect on student achievement, controlling for other factors. The effect is observable in models predicting mathematics achievement of third, fourth, eighth, and ninth graders.

Additional studies measuring student success in the subject area in which the teacher holds an advanced degree have been relatively consistent in their findings of a positive effect of teachers with advanced degrees on high school student achievement. Goldhaber and Brewer (2000) draw on nationally representative data provided in the National Educational Longitudinal Study of 1988 (NELS:88)[16] to estimate the impact of teachers who hold master's degrees on the mathematics achievement of high school students. This study demonstrates the importance of the subject area in which the degree was awarded. The researchers found that high school student achievement gains in mathematics were associated with students assigned to teachers who earned a master's degree in mathematics, controlling for student and teacher characteristics. No effect was evident in cases where the teachers had no advanced degree or where the degree was earned in a subject other than mathematics.

Rowan, Chiang, and Miller's (1997) analysis of the NELS:88 dataset further documents the importance of the subject matter of a teacher's degree for student mathematics achievement at the high school level. The model includes a variable indicating whether the teacher had majored in mathematics in undergraduate and/or graduate school. While the researchers did not distinguish the level of the degree earned, the subject-specific degree variable was a positive predictor of tenth-grade student achievement in all specifications of the model tested.

Goldhaber and Brewer (1998) further confirm the importance of subject-specific teacher preparation in drawing conclusions about the effect of teacher characteristics on teacher effectiveness. They analyzed NELS:88 data to address questions about when to monetarily reward teachers with advanced degrees. Their findings suggest that non-subject-specific teacher degrees are not related to high school student achievement in math, science, English, or history. However, in math and science, subject-specific degrees earned were found to have a positive impact on student test scores in those subjects. This was the case for both bachelor's and master's degrees. Further, teachers holding both a bachelor's and a master's degree in the subject area taught were the most effective.

Summary of findings on teacher preparation programs and degrees

The studies reviewed that pertain to the impact of teacher education programs and academic degrees on teacher effectiveness offer several insights. First, limited research has been conducted on the relationship between teacher education programs and teacher performance on the job, resulting in no strong evidence that teacher education programs, as a whole, contribute to teacher effectiveness. The research in this area tends to show that teachers learn professional knowledge and skills from these programs, but provides little evidence about the degree to which the learned skills contribute to teacher effectiveness.

Second, there is evidence that the selectivity or prestige of the institution attended by the teacher has a positive effect on student achievement. While the effect is most evident at the secondary level, a modest positive effect has been identified at the elementary level, and that effect has been shown to be most pronounced for low-income students. Some have argued that this measure of institutional selectivity is a reflection of teachers' cognitive ability.

Third, the evidence from a set of quasi-experimental studies controlling for student and teacher characteristics suggests that teachers who have earned an advanced degree have a positive impact on high school mathematics achievement and, to a lesser degree, science achievement, but only when the degree is earned in mathematics and science, respectively. In one study, this effect was limited to black students. A similar effect of advanced degrees on English and history achievement was not apparent at the high school level. Further, advanced degrees appear to have a negative effect, if any, on student achievement in the earlier grades. Also, while there is some evidence that extended teacher education programs can promote better recruitment and retention of teachers, there is no evidence that these programs have a positive impact on teacher performance.

Teacher certification

*Existing empirical studies reveal a positive effect of **subject-specific teacher certification** on high school mathematics achievement, but no statistically significant effect for elementary mathematics or reading. Studies of teachers who receive **emergency or alternative-route teacher certification** have shown little clear impact on student performance in high school mathematics and science, as compared to teachers who acquire certification through standard channels.*

Teacher certification has traditionally served as the primary gatekeeping mechanism for the teaching profession. The specific requirements for certification vary from state to state, but typically include completion of an accredited teacher education program, practice teaching, and a formal recommendation from the institution of higher education. Many states also require that teachers pass a certification test. There are several classifications of certification including regular or standard certification, provisional certification, advanced certification, alternative certification, and private school certification. A great deal of policy debate surrounds the type of certification teachers should possess and the appropriate balance between alternative and traditional routes to teacher certification. Research on these issues is described on the following pages.

Subject-specific certification

Hawk, Coble, and Swanson (1985) studied the effect on student achievement in mathematics of secondary teachers certified in mathematics versus those certified in other subjects. The study used a paired-comparison design, including a sample of 36 secondary school teachers—18 in-field (mathematics certified) and 18 out-of-field—and 826 students. Teachers were matched by the school where they were teaching, the mathematics courses they were teaching, and the ability level of their students. Outcomes were measured by scores on achievement tests in algebra and general mathematics. Researchers also tested for differences in knowledge of mathematics and professional skills in the classroom between in-field and out-of-field teachers. The researchers found that student achievement scores in both general mathematics and algebra were higher for students whose teachers were certified in mathematics. In addition, teachers certified in mathematics demonstrated greater knowledge of the subject and scored significantly higher on the instructional presentation component of the instrument measuring professional skills. Based on this study, it appears that teacher certification in mathematics has a positive impact on secondary school teacher performance and student achievement in mathematics.

Goldhaber and Brewer (1997a) conducted a more controlled multivariate analysis using the nationally representative NELS:88 data to investigate the impact of secondary school teacher certification on student achievement in mathematics. They found that students assigned to teachers who were certified in mathematics or who had earned a bachelor's or master's degree in mathematics had higher test scores than those assigned to teachers who lacked mathematics certification, controlling for other student and teacher characteristics. In contrast, they found that the mathematics scores of students assigned to teachers with master's degrees or certification in subjects other than mathematics were no different than scores of students assigned to teachers with fewer qualifications, further underlining the importance of subject-specific credentials, at least in high school mathematics.

The Rowan, Correnti, and Miller (2002) study described in the previous section provides evidence on the impact of teacher certification on elementary student achievement growth in mathematics and reading. This study used data from *Prospects: The Congressionally Mandated Study of Educational Opportunity* and hierarchical growth models that controlled for a variety of background factors to study the effect of teacher attributes on the performance of two student cohorts. The researchers found that subject-specific certification had no discernible impact on student achievement growth in mathematics or reading for either cohort.

Alternative-route certification

Given the contrast between teacher supply and demand, alternative teacher certification programs have become an important policy issue. Darling-Hammond (1990) distinguishes between alternative routes to certification, which do not change the standards but introduce other options for attaining them, and alternative certification, which changes the standards under which certification is granted. She argues that fully prepared and certified teachers are generally more highly rated than teachers without full preparation. Nevertheless, Hawley (1990) concludes that alternative certification programs will continue to emerge due to a number of factors, including the continuing teacher shortage in the context of high demand and the relatively low cost of some alternative certification programs.

Goldhaber and Brewer (2000) extended their analysis of the NELS:88 data to study the impact of different types of teacher certification on student achievement in high school mathematics and science. Based on their econometric analysis, they conclude that mathematics students whose teachers earned the standard certification do significantly better than students whose teachers hold private school certification or who are not certified in their subject area. In contrast, they found no evidence that mathematics and science students of teachers with emergency credentials do any worse than students whose teachers have standard teaching credentials.

But in a critique of the Goldhaber and Brewer study, Darling-Hammond et al. (2001) argued that the emergency certified teachers included in the study are most likely veteran teachers who hold some sort of licensure, for instance, those who have moved and are not fully certified in the state where they are teaching. As a result, she argues, these individuals are similarly qualified to teachers holding standard certification, so one would not expect to see a difference in the effect of these two groups on student achievement. In their original article, Goldhaber and Brewer (2000) noted that "individuals who hold emergency or private school certification likely have not come into the teaching profession through a conventional route. As a result these individuals have probably not received the same formal training" (p. 133).[17] The NELS:88 data do not provide more refined information on certification standards than the broad categories included in the Goldhaber and Brewer study, prohibiting a resolution to this dispute about emergency certification among NELS:88 teachers. In their rejoinder to the Darling-Hammond, et al. critique, Goldhaber and Brewer (2001) aptly defend their analysis and recognize the importance of getting more refined data on various teacher certification requirements to further cull the effects.

A number of additional studies, most using some form of matched-comparison design, have shown little or no difference between teachers with standard certification versus those with alternative certification. Hawk and Schmidt (1989) compared 19 alternatively certified teachers with 53 teachers holding standard certification and found that the two groups were almost equally successful on several dimensions of the National Teaching Examination. While the alternatively certified teachers were as likely as those holding standard certification to meet standards for teaching practices, the alternatively certified teachers were less likely to exceed those standards. This study did not control for background characteristics of the two groups of teachers.

Lutz and Hutton (1989) studied 100 alternatively certified teachers across all grade levels and found that they were rated as high or higher by their principals and mentor teachers than were first-year teachers with standard certification. The alternatively certified teachers also scored as high or higher on standardized measures of teaching performance. Again, no controls were used in this study.

Guyton, Fox, and Sisk (1991) compared 23 alternatively certified teachers with 26 teachers from standard certification programs on a number of measures including teacher attitudes, teacher self-evaluations of performance, and principal or mentor's evaluation of the teacher's performance. The two groups of teachers were similar in characteristics such as subject area taught, gender, and socioeconomic status. In addition, the school characteristics of the two groups of teachers were comparable in terms of the type of community (rural, urban, suburban), economic conditions of the community, school size, average student ability level, administrative support, racial composition, and teacher attrition. The researchers found that alternatively certified teachers and teachers from standard certification programs were similar on almost all measures. The alternatively certified teachers expressed more positive feelings about the value of their teacher education programs, while the teachers with standard certification felt more positive about teaching at the end of the school year and were more enthusiastic about remaining in the teaching profession.

In their study of 300 alternatively certified teachers in grades K-12, Stafford and Barrow (1994) reported that principals were generally pleased with the work of alternatively certified interns and felt that the abilities of interns were similar to those of other first-year teachers.[18] The researchers found no difference in student achievement between the two groups at the secondary level.

Miller, McKenna, and McKenna (1998) conducted a paired-comparison analysis of 82 fifth- and sixth-grade teachers (41 with standard certification and 41 with alternative certification). The two groups of teachers were similar in terms of years of experience, subject and grade level taught, and school where they worked. Based on their analysis, the researchers concluded that alternative certification did not lead to inferior teaching practices. Further, the researchers found no difference in student achievement scores or teachers' perceptions of their own teaching ability across the two groups of teachers.

The only study meeting the selection criteria for this analysis that found negative effects associated with alternative teacher certification is McDiarmid and Wilson (1991). They studied 55 elementary and secondary mathematics teachers; all of the individuals in the sample had earned undergraduate degrees in mathematics and subsequently participated in alternative certification programs. Based on questionnaire and interview data regarding teachers' abilities to help students learn and understand mathematics, the researchers concluded that teachers entering the profession through alternative routes may be poorly prepared to help students develop an understanding of mathematics, particularly at the elementary school level.

Finally, an article by Darling-Hammond (1990) draws on literature in order to "get underneath the surface of [the debate over teacher education programs], assessing the design and potential outcomes of alternate route programs with reference to their perspectives and assumptions about teaching knowledge, teacher preparation, and their relationship to student learning" (p. 124). This article reviewed studies that examined the relationship between teacher education and teacher effectiveness and found that all reviews of this relationship conclude that fully prepared and certified teachers are generally more highly rated and more successful with students than teachers without full preparation. Further, Darling-Hammond argues that teachers admitted through quick-entry alternative routes are frequently noted to have difficulty along a number of dimensions (e.g., curriculum development, pedagogical content knowledge, attending to students' differing learning styles, motivation, and language arts achievement). These conclusions, coupled with the majority of findings presented above that report no difference between regular and alternatively certified teachers, suggest that more attention needs to be paid to this issue, particularly to what the various approaches to certification entail.

Summary of findings on teacher certification
The range of empirical studies of teacher certification demonstrates a positive effect of certified teachers on high school mathematics achievement when the certification is in mathematics. This subject-specific certification effect is not observable in other high school subjects or in elementary-level mathematics or reading. Further, studies have shown little clear impact (either positive or negative) of emergency or alternative-route certification teachers on student performance in mathematics and science relative to teachers acquiring certification through standard channels.

Teacher coursework

Studies of middle and high school education (primarily mathematics and science) reveal that **coursework in both pedagogy and content areas** *has a positive impact of student achievement. With respect to grade level, the evidence indicates that, although pedagogical coursework seems to contribute to teacher effectiveness at all grade levels, the importance of coursework in content areas is most apparent at the secondary level. Further, evidence suggests that the effect of content coursework of high school teachers may taper off at some point (e.g., after five courses for high school math teachers), while the effect of pedagogical coursework persists, and may even outweigh that associated with content coursework.*

A set of interpretive studies conclude that **field experiences as a component of teacher coursework** *tend to be disconnected from the other com-*

ponents of teacher education programs. Despite this, studies suggest positive effects in terms of opportunities to learn the profession and reduced anxiety among new teachers.

Measures of the level and type of coursework taken by teachers represent proxies for what teachers know and can do in the sense that coursework indicates the degree of exposure individuals have had to particular areas of study. Studies on this topic explore two basic categories: the amount of coursework taken in particular areas (e.g., education courses versus subject-matter courses) and the contribution of field experiences such as student teaching. The issue of the appropriate mix of coursework in teacher preparation programs is a recurrent theme in many teacher policy proposals over the past two decades (see chapter one). The research on both types of teacher coursework is considered below.

Amount and type of coursework

As noted by Ferguson and Womack (1993), "During the mid-1980s the debate over the importance of subject matter versus education coursework in teacher preparation programs took on new life" (p. 55). An early analysis of science teacher preparation by Perkes (1967) explored the relationship between student achievement and the amount of academic work by junior high school science teachers in science and related subjects. Teacher preparation was measured by the amount of academic coursework in science, coursework in science education, grade point average in science, and recency of coursework. On the outcome side, distinctions were made between students' ability to recall factual knowledge and their ability to apply that knowledge. The sample for the study included 32 general science teachers and 3,062 students enrolled in general science courses from one suburban school district. Correlational relationships were the basis for the findings reported, so no causal conclusions can be drawn from the analysis. Nonetheless, several interesting findings are worth noting here. First, the number of credits teachers earned in science was not markedly related to either student outcome variable, even after stratifying the sample by gender and level of intelligence (as measured by I.Q. scores). Second, teachers' coursework in science education and their grade point averages in science courses were both significantly and positively correlated with students' abilities to apply their science knowledge and inversely related to measures of students' abilities to recall factual knowledge. Thus, both coursework in science education and grade point averages in science courses appear to positively affect students' abilities to apply science knowledge, but diminish their abilities to recall science facts. To the extent that a teacher's science grade point average is a measure of science content knowledge, these findings suggest that both content and pedagogical knowledge contribute to teacher effectiveness. The researchers also provide some evidence that the recency of the college science coursework is important. Recent enrollment in a college-level course was found to be a positive predictor of student achievement. Finally, teachers with more science education credits used discussion and laboratory principles and stressed application of ideas, while teachers with fewer credits in science education placed greater emphasis on students' memorization of facts. This finding may explain how and why methodology courses influence teacher effectiveness. Further, these findings are consistent with studies discussed in the section on teacher education programs that indicate that subject-specific pedagogical training is a critical component of teacher preparation (Grossman 1989; Grossman et al. 2003; Hollingsworth 1989).

Nelson and Wood (1985) studied 94 student teachers divided into groups based on supervisors' ratings of their student teaching performance. The researchers found a statistically significant difference between the high- and low-performing teachers in terms of their prior performance in pedagogical courses. They conclude, "It would appear that as the content of coursework more closely relates to the knowledge and skills required in teaching, performance in that coursework can more reliably predict success in student teaching and subsequently (it is assumed) in teaching" (p. 56). This study did not identify the level of education or subject areas for which the teachers were prepared, and the lack of controls limit causal inferences from this analysis.

Eberts and Stone's (1984) quasi-experimental study of public education includes measures of teacher course-taking in its multivariate model that predicts the impact of teacher characteristics on mathematics achievement gains among fourth-grade students. Specifically, the researchers include a variable indicating the number of college-level mathematics courses taken by teachers in the last three years. Controlling for student background and other teacher characteristics (including in-service training in the last three years), the researchers found no statistically significant effect of teachers' recent mathematics coursework on student achievement.

Ferguson and Womack (1993) assessed the extent to which education and subject-matter coursework predict the teaching performance of student teachers completing one university's teacher education program. In this study, teaching performance was measured by 107 survey items that assessed 13 categories of teacher expertise. Independent variables of interest were amount of education coursework, grade point average in the student's major, and National Teacher Examination (NTE) specialty scores.

The latter two are interpreted by the researchers to represent measures of content knowledge. The sample of teachers included 266 secondary student teachers over a seven-semester period between 1988 and 1991. Data were analyzed using analysis of variance and stepwise regression. The researchers found that the proportion of variance in teacher performance explained by the amount of education coursework taken was 16.5%. In contrast, measures of content (in-major grade point average and NTE specialty score) explained less than 4% of the variance in teacher performance. These results suggest that education coursework is a more powerful predictor of teaching effectiveness than measures of content expertise as indicated by grade point average and NTE specialty scores. Further, the researchers' conclusions were consistent with what they found in the literature on the subject: "while subject-matter knowledge is an important prerequisite for effective teaching, it is not sufficient in and of itself and knowledge beyond that typically required for certification does not result in increasing the quality of teaching performance" (p. 56).

Monk (1994) drew on more refined measures of teacher coursework to examine the impact of various types of teacher preparation on student achievement in mathematics and science. In addition, he compared the effects of teacher coursework with the effects of more conventional measures like experience and degree level. Teacher preparation was measured by the number of courses teachers took in various areas (i.e., mathematics content, science content, mathematics education, science education) and at different levels (i.e., undergraduate and graduate). In addition, the type of course (i.e., mathematics, life science, physical science) was considered to address the possible importance of matching teacher preparation with teacher assignment. Data for this study came from the Longitudinal Study of American Youth (LSAY), a nationally representative panel survey including a base-year sample of 2,829 students from 51 randomly selected public high schools. This study found that the amount of content preparation that teachers have is positively associated with student achievement in high school mathematics and science, and that this effect depends on the subject being taught, the characteristics of the students being taught (e.g., advanced versus remedial), and additional teacher attributes. Monk reports a curvilinear relationship between subject-matter teacher preparation and student gains; for example, after taking five mathematics courses, each additional math course beyond five has a smaller effect on pupil performance compared to the effect of an additional mathematics course up to and including the fifth course. In addition, teacher coursework in pedagogy was found to contribute positively to student learning and sometimes had more powerful effects than additional preparation in content areas. On this matter, Monk concludes, a "good grasp of one's subject area is a necessary but not a sufficient condition for effective teaching" (p. 142). Finally, Monk found that in contrast to course-taking variables, conventional measures (degree level, undifferentiated credit counts, and experience) tended to be either unrelated or negatively related to improvements in pupil performance.

Monk and King (1994) explored the effects of secondary mathematics and science teachers' subject-matter preparation on the performance gains of their pupils in these subjects. This study also drew on data from the LSAY and used hierarchical linear models. The researchers hypothesized that the effects of teacher preparation are likely to exist at multiple levels within schools. They took account for this by distinguishing between the teachers that a student was assigned to in the classroom and the other teachers that contributed to education schoolwide. The results suggest that it is the cumulative effect of the set of teachers a student has had over time, rather than the subject-matter preparation of the entire faculty in the school, that affects student mathematics and science achievement. Further, results were found to depend on the type of student (high versus low pretest), and subject matter (mathematics versus science).

Druva and Anderson's (1983) meta-analysis of research on the relationship between science teacher characteristics (including course-taking) and student achievement found that the number of biology courses taken by biology teachers and the number of science courses taken are both positively associated with student achievement. In addition, the importance of pedagogical coursework versus content coursework is underlined in several reviews of this literature. Evertson, Hawley, and Zlotnik (1985) find a consistent positive effect of the pedagogical component of teacher preparation programs, but report mixed results regarding the impact of coursework in the subject area they teach. Ashton and Crocker (1987) review the literature on the effect of the amount of coursework taken by teachers in professional education compared to coursework taken in academic education. They find four of seven estimates (57%) of the impact of professional education to be significantly positive, compared to only five of 14 (36%) for academic education. Likewise, Darling-Hammond (1990) reviewed studies examining the influence of subject-matter and education courses on teacher effectiveness. While the positive impact of education courses shows up "consistently and strongly," subject-matter knowledge contributes to good teaching only up to a certain point, beyond which it does not seem to have an impact. In other words, past the level of basic subject-area preparation, most research found that additional study of teaching methods has a stronger influence on teacher effectiveness than additional subject-matter preparation.

Field experiences

Several studies have also explored the importance of student-teaching experiences in predicting subsequent teaching performance. In general, these studies fall into the interpretive tradition and tend to involve small samples of teachers. One key finding across a number of studies is that field experiences tend to be disconnected from the other components of teacher education programs, leaving teachers poorly equipped to apply their knowledge from classroom coursework to teaching in the field. Goodman's (1985) case study of 10 preservice teachers attending an elementary education program at a large southeastern university sheds light on what students learn from early field experiences. The study concludes that more time should be spent by student teachers in a single context and that university field supervisors need to emphasize connections between theory and practice to encourage instructional experimentation among student teachers.

Clift's (1991) interpretive analysis of a single teacher majoring in English at a large urban university highlights the multiple schemata that this teacher drew upon as she began to interact with students in the classroom. Further, the researcher concludes that these schemata are not equally developed and are difficult to integrate as the teacher worked to apply her knowledge to a practical situation.

Eisenhart, Belm, and Romagnano (1991) studied eight preservice middle school mathematics teachers who were completing a year-long student teaching experience. The student teaching involved four assignments per teacher (two each semester); during three of these placements, students taught for half of the day and took methods courses during the second half. The eight student teachers, the program director, and the methods instructors were interviewed and observed. The researchers report that the participants found the program to be uncoordinated and incoherent. The students found their coursework, including previous subject-area and general education courses as well as the methods courses taken alongside the student teaching, to be too theoretical and of limited use in the classroom.

Shulman's (1987) interpretive study of student teaching focused on a ninth-grade preservice English teacher attending a large midwestern university, and also included a cooperating teacher and two other student teachers who served as validating informants. Shulman found during the course of the year that the student teacher experienced many emotions typical of student teachers, including both positive feelings of success as well as negative feelings of frustration and despair. A particular problem in this case was the "hands-off" nature of the cooperating teacher who offered little guidance or support. While the student teacher's task may have been made easier with more training in teacher education, by the end of the student-teaching experience she had made strides both in terms of her rapport with students and her grasp of the curriculum.

An analysis by Griffin (1989) is the only instance of a large-scale, multi-site study of student teaching. This study participants included 93 student teachers, 88 cooperating teachers, and 17 university supervisors. Data included personality constructs, cognitive measures, outcomes, program components, site characteristics, and the nature and content of participants' interactions over a semester of student teaching. The overarching purpose of the study was to describe the student-teaching experience in terms of the characteristics and behaviors of cooperating teachers, student teachers, and university supervisors. Among the findings described in the article, the authors report that participants were generally satisfied with their experiences. Further, the student teachers were rated highly in terms of carrying out their responsibilities, though the high ratings were accompanied by low variability, suggesting that either the teacher candidates were all exemplary or that the instrument needs to be refined so that it can more effectively discriminate among the teachers. However, the researchers conclude that the student-teaching program was only minimally related to the university teacher education programs, and that there were few links between the university and the public schools to which the teachers were assigned. Finally, the lack of clear performance standards undermined the clarity of the program.

Several studies suggest that field experiences contribute to the knowledge base and professional learning that teacher candidates develop during their preparation programs. Grossman and Richert's (1988) interviews with 12 teachers suggest that coursework and fieldwork offer distinct opportunities for student teachers to learn the profession. Silvernail and Costello's (1983) study of 24 student teachers found that these individuals report that student internship programs are effective in reducing preservice teachers' teaching anxiety and may be beneficial. The findings of Pigge (1978) and Clark, Smith, Newby, and Cook (1985) reviewed earlier also imply an important role for applied field experiences as part of teacher education programs. While all of these studies attest to the importance of field experiences in teacher preparation programs, no controlled studies of causal relationships between field experiences and teacher actual performance could be found.

Summary of findings on teacher coursework
The studies reviewed in this section vary in terms of the measures, data, and methods used. Nonetheless, they are relatively consistent in their find-

ings. Most notably, they suggest that teacher coursework in both content areas and pedagogy contributes to positive educational outcomes, but the relative impact of their effect varies. Subject-matter preparation in the subject area taught is shown to be important at the high school level, but investments here appear to have diminishing returns after the first several courses. Coursework in education methods, especially those that couple pedagogy with the subject matter (e.g., math education courses), is shown to have consistent positive effects that often outweigh those of content coursework. Several of the more sophisticated multivariate studies reviewed here demonstrate some of the complexities associated with the education production process. More specifically, the effect of teacher qualifications appears to depend on a number of factors including student characteristics, teacher attributes, and subject area. With respect to grade level, the studies included in this review offer some evidence that, while pedagogical coursework seems to contribute to teacher effectiveness at all grade levels, the importance of coursework in content areas is most pronounced at the secondary level. This conclusion echoes the findings presented in the previous section that the impact of advanced degrees and certification on teacher effectiveness is highest at the secondary level.

Although the studies on the field experience component of teacher education are not designed to reveal causal relationships, they offer several insights. A set of interpretive studies concludes that field experiences tend to be disconnected from the other components of teacher education programs. Despite this, evidence suggests that field experiences such as student teaching have positive effects in terms of opportunity to learn the profession and reduced anxiety among new teachers.

Teacher test scores

The studies reviewed in this section suggest that some test scores predict levels of teacher performance and desired educational outcomes. More specifically, tests that assess the literacy levels or verbal abilities of teachers tend to show positive effects. In contrast, studies of the impact of the National Teacher Examination and other state-mandated tests of basic skills and/or teaching abilities report mixed findings. Finally, the studies presented here also reinforce the complexity of the education production process in that the effects of what teachers know and can do as indicated by test scores depend on factors like student and teacher attributes. In particular, evidence suggests that teacher test scores matter most for educationally at-risk students.

Teachers' scores on tests are arguably one of the best indicators of what teachers know and can do because they go beyond measuring exposure to programs and specific courses to actually assessing the knowledge and skills that individuals have acquired.[19] Teacher assessments are also interesting from a policy perspective. While policy makers can require that certain tests be taken and passed by teacher candidates, it is far more difficult to influence the degree to which a given set of individuals will excel on these tests, particularly broad proficiency assessments such as literacy tests. One solution is for policies aimed at increasing teacher quality as indicated by test scores to require that teacher salaries be raised enough to spur an increase in teacher supply so that districts could select teachers with higher test scores.

The debate over the role and relevance of teacher test scores received a great deal of attention in the late 1970s and through the 1980s. One explanation for this may be that the legality of using the National Teacher Examination (NTE) for certification purposes was upheld by the United States Supreme Court in NEA v. South Carolina in 1978 (Stedman 1984). More recently, the federal Teacher Quality Enhancement Grants for States and Partnerships (Title II) legislation requires states to issue "report cards" on their teacher tests and licensure policies in order to hold states and higher education institutions accountable for the quality of teacher preparation. Teacher testing is included as part of the licensure requirements of 42 states, and a variety of teacher assessments have been developed for this purpose (National Research Council 2001; Latham, Gitomer, and, Ziomek 1999). Ferguson (1998) demonstrates that certification testing "reduces the number of people who enter the profession with weak basic skills…and is probably helping to narrow the gap between black and white students" (p. 351). An increasingly popular evaluation is the portfolio assessment by the National Board of Professional Teaching Standards, which recognizes accomplished teachers with national certification.

Given the widespread practice of testing teachers, the U.S. Department of Education requested that the National Academy of Sciences create a Committee on Assessment and Teacher Quality. This committee was asked to examine the appropriateness and technical quality of teacher licensure tests currently in use. The resulting National Research Council report (NRC 2001) proposes 12 criteria for evaluating teacher tests, and applied these criteria to the evaluation of current Praxis teacher assessments. The criteria include consideration of: (1) the purpose of the assessment; (2) the competencies to be assessed; (3) the development of the assessment; (4) field testing and exercise analysis; (5) administration and scoring; (6) protection from corruptibility; (7) standard setting, (8) consistency, reliability, generalizability, and comparability; (9) score reporting and documentation; (10) validation studies; (11) cost and feasibility; and (12) long-term consequences of a licensure program.

While the Praxis tests evaluated in the NRC report met many of these criteria, the criterion of most interest for the purpose of this review is the existence and findings of validation studies. Most of the teacher tests examined in the report had been the object of validation studies, but these studies were primarily based on content-related evidence that examines the degree to which the test adequately represents the content needed to perform the tasks and duties required of the job. Based on their analysis, the NRC report authors state that "Few, if any [test] developers are collecting evidence about how test results relate to other relevant measures of candidates' knowledge, skills, and abilities" (p. 6). The authors strongly recommend more concerted efforts to study the validity of teacher tests using criterion-based evidence such as systematic classroom observation, portfolios, or comparisons of teacher performance among those who pass these tests with those who do not. The remainder of this section reviews studies that have examined the relationship between teacher tests and measures of their knowledge and skills.

National Teacher Examination

Given the historical role of the NTE as a gatekeeper for the teaching profession, the predictive validity of this instrument has been the focus of study across the past three decades. A number of studies have examined the relationship between NTE scores and teacher performance and competence. An early review by Quirk, Witten, and Weinberg (1973) examined studies of the relationship between teachers' NTE scores and their undergraduate grades, practice teaching grades, and ratings by supervisors of their on-the-job teaching. The researchers identified 16 correlations between teacher test scores and their grade point averages, ranging in value from 0.23 to 0.74, with a median of 0.55 (a moderate relationship). Two correlations between teacher scores and practice teaching grades were reported, with values that were close to zero. Finally, the researchers identified six correlations between teachers' test scores and their teaching performance, as indicated by supervisor ratings. These values ranged from -0.15 to 0.45, with a median of 0.11 (a weak relationship).

Since that time, a number of additional correlational studies have been conducted that find a weak relationship, if any, between teachers' NTE scores and their performance. While Ayers and Qualls (1979) found that NTE scores are significantly related to teacher candidates' grade point averages and scores on the ACT, correlations between NTE scores and teacher performance as measured by principal and pupil ratings were found to be quite low and generally not statistically significant. The only exception was a statistically significant correlation between teachers' scores and principals' ratings of secondary teachers' subject-matter competency.

Likewise, Piper and O'Sullivan (1981) demonstrate that NTE scores are not highly correlated with supervisor ratings during the student-teaching period or during the first year of teaching. Similarly, Dorby, Murphy, and Schmidt's (1985) study of 45 student teachers found no statistically significant relationship between NTE professional knowledge scores and measures of student-teacher competence. Ayers' (1988) study of 48 education graduates found that while scores from the NTE were significantly correlated with ACT scores and mean grade point average, in general, correlations between NTE scores and principal ratings of teaching performance were low. Andrews, Blackmon, and Mackey (1980) examined correlations among undergraduate grade point average, student teacher performance, and NTE scores for 269 student teachers. The researchers found a relationship between performance on the NTE and students' grade point averages. They concluded that the "NTE is valid for what is taught in the classroom but not necessarily for predicting teacher performance, a conclusion in keeping with the NTE literature" (p. 359).

In terms of student achievement as the outcome, Lawrenz's (1975) analysis of 236 secondary science teachers revealed that teachers' subject knowledge as measured by the NTE was negatively related to student achievement. However, this study was based on correlational analysis with no controls, so causal inferences are not appropriate.

The findings from multivariate studies designed to draw causal inferences about the relationship between teacher performance on the NTE and student achievement are mixed. Summers and Wolfe's (1977) analysis of factors related to student achievement in urban schools reveal interesting findings about the impact of teacher NTE scores on student performance at different levels of education. For their sample of 627 sixth graders, the researchers found a negative effect of teacher NTE scores on student achievement, controlling for a variety of student, teacher, and classroom variables. In contrast, the researchers found no evidence of a statistically significant effect for either the 553 eighth graders or the 717 twelfth graders in the study.

Sheehan and Marcus (1978) studied 119 first-grade teachers and 1,836 first-grade students in a large urban school district to estimate the effect of teachers' NTE scores on student achievement in mathematics and vocabulary. Controlling for student pretest scores and several teacher characteristics (e.g., degree, years of experience), the researchers found that teachers with higher NTE scores were associated with higher levels of student achievement in mathematics and vocabulary. However, when teacher race was controlled, the magnitudes of the contributions of the NTE scores were no longer statistically significant predictors of student math and vocabulary achievement.

Strauss and Sawyer (1986) studied the impact of teacher quality, as measured by the NTE standardized test scores, on student performance in terms of failure rates and academic achievement, controlling for a set of district characteristics (e.g., size, number of students interested in attending college, number of black students, number of teachers). Based on data from 145 school districts in a single state, the researchers found that a 1% increase in teacher quality as measured by NTE scores is accompanied by a 5% decline in the failure rate of students on standardized competency tests. The corresponding impact on average student achievement is less dramatic, but arguably still policy relevant: the elasticity of teacher quality with respect to student reading and mathematics test scores ranges between 0.5 and 0.8. That is, a 1% improvement in teacher quality as measured by NTE scores yields between 0.5% and 0.8% increase in mean student scores on math and reading tests. Further, the racial composition of the district appears to be an important factor. The authors state, "Of the inputs which are potentially policy-controllable (teacher quality, teacher numbers via the pupil-teacher ratio, and capital stock) our analysis indicates quite clearly that improving the quality of teachers in the classroom will do more for students who are most educationally at risk, those prone to fail, than reducing class size or improving the capital stock by any reasonable margin which would be available to policy makers" (p. 47).

Other tests of basic skills or general knowledge
In addition to research examining the relationship between the NTE and teacher performance, researchers have used a wide variety of assessments to study the impact of teacher test scores on teacher effectiveness. Guyton and Farokhi (1987) analyzed the degree to which the academic quality of teachers in terms of their basic skills, subject-matter knowledge, and academic performance is related to teaching performance. The study sample included graduates of teacher education programs at one university. All individuals included in the study had available test scores for either of two statewide tests, one for basic skills (n = 413) and the other for subject-matter knowledge (n = 273). These teacher test scores served as the measure of the academic quality of teachers. In addition, teachers' sophomore and upper-level grade point averages were used to indicate academic performance. The outcome variable, teaching performance, was measured with the Teacher Per-

formance Assessment Instrument, which assesses on-the-job performance of all beginning teachers in the state. Simple correlations were the basis for the analysis. The analysis revealed that neither the scores on the test of basic skills nor those on the test of subject-matter knowledge were significantly related to teacher performance. However, academic performance, as measured by teacher grade point average, was found to be positively related to teaching performance. High performance in upper-level courses was found to have the strongest effect, and in this state, education methods are taught in those upper level courses. Consequently, the authors conclude, "It may be that academic performance in education courses is the best predictor of teaching success...what is contradicted [by these findings] is the idea that a person well grounded in an academic discipline would be able to teach well with little or no pedagogical education" (p. 40). This conclusion is consistent with the findings presented in the section on the effects of teacher coursework.

The more recent studies of the impact of teacher test scores are quantitative, multivariate analyses that control for a variety of student, teacher, and school characteristics, allowing for causal inferences to be drawn. Ehrenberg and Brewer (1995) reanalyzed data from the 1966 report *Equality of Educational Opportunity* to study whether teacher characteristics such as verbal ability and race affect student achievement as measured by estimated gain scores. This multivariate analysis revealed that the verbal aptitude scores of teachers influenced students' synthetic gain scores. Teachers' test scores were found to be a positive predictor of student achievement gains at both the elementary level (third-grade score subtracted from the fifth-grade score) and secondary level (ninth-grade score subtracted from the twelfth-grade score). This effect was present for both white and black students, and the impact mattered as much for black teachers as white.

In contrast, in their study of effective elementary teachers of inner-city black children, Murnane and Phillips (1981) found no evidence of a statistically significant relationship between teacher verbal ability scores, as measured on a self-administered test, and student vocabulary achievement in grades three, four, or five after controlling for a variety of student and teacher characteristics. The researchers found a negative effect of teachers' verbal ability on sixth-grade student achievement, which they dismissed as spurious, because the researchers describe, "a large number of teachers used aids in completing the test" (p. 97-98). This study was based on data on approximately 200 black students at each grade level in one urban school district and included controls for a variety of student and teacher background characteristics.

Two analyses conducted by Ferguson (1991, 1998) provide evidence of a positive relationship between teacher performance on tests of verbal ability and teacher effectiveness, as measured by student achievement. Ferguson's studies are based on Texas data that include 150,000 teachers in more than 800 school districts. Controlling for a variety of student, teacher, and school characteristics, Ferguson (1991) finds that the average teacher score across a school district is a positive predictor of student reading gains in grades five, seven, nine, and 11 in that district. The finding of a positive effect is also presented in Ferguson (1998), where the argument is made that testing teachers may contribute to narrowing the achievement gap between black and white students.

Based on data from 29,544 students in Alabama, Ferguson and Ladd (1996) estimated the effect of teachers' performance on the ACT on student reading and mathematics achievement gains from third to fourth grade and from eighth to ninth grade. The analysis controlled for a variety of student and teacher variables. At the school level, the researchers found a positive relationship between teacher test score and student achievement gains for the younger sample in reading, but not mathematics. The district-level analysis revealed a positive relationship between the average teacher ACT score in the district and average mathematics achievement gain in the district for both younger and older students.

Finally, Rowan, Chiang, and Miller's (1997) model predicting tenth graders' mathematics achievement based on data from NELS:88 found a positive effect of teachers' mathematics quiz scores on student achievement gains in mathematics.[20] This effect was found after controlling for student and teacher background variables, including whether teachers held mathematics-related degrees.

Summary of findings on teacher test scores

The studies reviewed in this section suggest that some test scores seem to predict teacher performance and educational outcomes. More specifically, tests that assess the impact of literacy levels or verbal abilities of teachers tend to show positive effects on student achievement. In contrast, studies of the impact of the NTE and other state-mandated tests of basic skills and/ or teaching abilities report mixed findings. Finally, all of these studies reinforce the complexity of the education production process in that the effects of what teachers know and can do as indicated by test scores depend on factors such as student and teacher attributes. In particular, evidence suggests that teacher test scores matter most for educationally at-risk students.

CHAPTER 4

Summary of the literature and implications for policy and research

Teacher quality is important. Given the high costs coupled with the high impact, this educational element has profound implications for the efficiency, equity, and adequacy of public education.

Teacher policy should reflect an appropriate balance between "professionalization" and "deregulation" and be guided by the evidence of effectiveness where such evidence is robust. Efforts to improve the stock of high-quality teachers should recognize the context of teaching. This analysis suggests that teacher policy and practice should reflect the variable needs of elementary schools, high schools, subject areas, and disadvantaged students.

While some current teacher policies and practices are supported by research, many are based on thin or no evidence. More research is needed in order inform policy making in a manner that provides good investment outcomes specific to the setting, student characteristics, teacher characteristics, and individual teaching responsibilities.

This report set out to distill the evidence on the relationship between teacher attributes generally assumed to be related to quality and teacher performance. Volumes have been written on the issue of teacher quality; the purpose of this report was to digest the findings from the diverse array of empirical studies in a way that can inform debates about how we define and recognize teacher quality. A clearer understanding of what the evidence really shows about teacher quality is necessary to evaluate, reconsider, and adjust assumptions underlying current teacher hiring, compensation, and distribution practices. Arguably, this sort of empirically grounded approach is needed to guide policy decisions about how to best invest limited resources to improve teacher quality.

In general, the wide range of studies reviewed here suggests several broad conclusions regarding teacher quality. These conclusions, however, should be interpreted in light of the availability of empirical evidence. A conclusion that there is no evidence of a particular relationship does *not necessarily* mean that there is not a relationship. Rather, it means that no relationship has been identified in empirical analyses, that the existing empirical findings are mixed, or that the particular relationship has not been studied. The findings presented here describe what conclusions can be drawn from the existing research. This includes demonstrated relationships (both positive and negative), as well as instances where the relationship was studied but no convincing evidence could be found.

Of course, conclusions can only be based on what has actually been studied. So, for example, the finding that high school teacher certification in mathematics has a positive effect on math achievement tells us nothing about the impact of certification in other subjects or at other grade levels. The following bullets summarize the findings of the empirical evidence, identifying the particular subjects and the level of education where relevant. The remainder of this chapter is devoted to highlighting some of the broader observations and limitations of this work and describing a set of implications for policy.

Summary and discussion of the findings

The findings described below are organized by the five categories of teacher quality indicators.

Teacher experience

- A set of quasi-experimental studies designed to test the causal relationship between teacher experience and student achievement reveals a positive relationship between these two variables. At the elementary level, this relationship is most evident during the first several years of teaching, and there is some evidence that positive effects reemerge among very experienced teachers (more than 14 years). Estimates of the effect of teacher experience on high school student achievement suggest that experience has a more sustained effect, continuing later into teachers' careers.

Teacher preparation programs and degrees

- Primarily qualitative in nature, the studies of *teacher education programs* reveal mixed evidence regarding the degree to which these programs contribute to teachers' knowledge. Several studies identify the specific components of teacher education programs that are most important (e.g., subject-specific pedagogy, classroom management). These studies offer limited evidence regarding the contribution of teacher education programs to teacher competencies or, more importantly, student achievement.

- In terms of the *selectivity/prestige of the higher education institutions* attended by teachers, the evidence suggests a modest positive effect of institutional selectivity on student performance at the elementary level, and a more significant positive effect at the high school level. Evidence also suggests that, at the elementary level, the positive effect of teacher quality, as indicated by the selectivity of the institution they attended, may be more pronounced for low-income students.

- Studies of *extended teacher education* programs suggest positive effects on the number of teachers entering the profession and teacher retention rates, but no clear effect on teacher performance, at least as indicated by principal evaluations.

- A number of quasi-experimental studies have been conducted on the impact of a teacher's *advanced degree on teacher effectiveness*. These studies have a history of showing no positive effect on student achievement, and sometimes even have negative effects for elementary student achievement. However, a recent wave of studies that take into consideration the subject area of the degree and teaching assignment have found a positive effect of subject-specific advanced degrees on student achievement. These studies are limited to high school mathematics and, to a lesser extent, science. In one study, this positive effect was limited to black students.

Teacher certification

- Existing empirical studies have demonstrated a positive effect of certified teachers on high school mathematics achievement when the certification is in mathematics. This *subject-specific teacher certification* effect is less obvious in other high school subject areas, and the effect is zero or even negative in elementary-level math and reading.

- Studies of *emergency or alternative-route teacher certification* have shown little clear impact on student performance in high school mathematics and science relative to teacher certification acquired through standard channels.

Teacher coursework

- Studies of middle and high school education (primarily mathematics and science) reveal that coursework in both pedagogy and content areas has a positive impact of student achievement. With respect to grade level, the evidence indicates that, while pedagogical coursework seems to contribute to teacher effectiveness at all grade levels, the importance of coursework in content areas is most apparent at the secondary level. Further, evidence suggests that the impact of content coursework on effectiveness of high school teachers may taper off after a certain amount of coursework is taken (e.g., after five courses for high school math teachers); however, the effect of pedagogical coursework persists and may even outweigh that associated with content coursework.

- A set of interpretive studies concludes that *field experiences* tend to be disconnected from the other components of teacher education programs. Despite this, studies suggest positive effects in terms of opportunity to learn the profession and reduced anxiety among new teachers.

Teacher test scores

- The studies reviewed in this section suggest that some test scores seem to predict levels of teacher performance and desired educational outcomes. More specifically, tests that assess the impact of literacy levels or verbal abilities of teachers tend to show positive effects. In contrast, studies of the impact of the National Teacher Examination and other state-mandated tests of basic skills and/or teaching abilities report mixed findings. Finally, all of the studies reviewed also reinforce the complexity of the education production process in that the effects of what teachers know and can do as indicated by test scores depend on factors like student and teacher attributes. In particular, evidence suggests that teacher test scores matter most for educationally at-risk students.

Taken together, the studies reviewed provide evidence that more refined measures of what teachers know and can do (e.g., subject-specific credentials, specific coursework taken) are better predictors of teacher and student performance than are more conventional measures (e.g., highest degree earned, undifferentiated course credits earned). This finding underlines the importance of going beyond broadly defined variables like Hanushek's (1997) "teacher education" to get a clearer sense of what really matters.

In addition, these studies reveal the interactive nature of various teacher qualities and qualifications. Consider, for instance, subject-matter knowledge of teachers. Much policy emphasis has been placed on the subject-matter preparation of teachers. While the studies reviewed here show that content knowledge is important, particularly for secondary school teachers, these findings generally link content knowledge with other qualifications (e.g., certification, degree, pedagogical coursework). In other words, it appears that having subject-matter expertise is necessary, but not sufficient. A number of studies, particularly those examining teacher preparation programs and coursework, suggest that teachers must learn and practice how to apply that knowledge in classroom settings, implying an important role for pedagogical training. At the high school level, these pedagogy courses should be linked with the subject matter taught, but these conclusions are limited to mathematics and, to a lesser degree, science.

A third general conclusion from this literature review is that teaching context matters in interpreting the evidence on the relationship between teacher attributes and their effectiveness. The studies reviewed here demonstrate that teacher qualities and qualifications are not equally effective across levels of education, subject areas, or types of students and classrooms. Perhaps the most consistent and compelling finding in this regard is the importance of subject-specific training and credentials for high school mathematics teachers. This finding appears with respect to high school teachers' degrees, certification, and coursework. The effect of subject-specific training and credentials is less apparent, and sometimes even negative, for elementary education. There is also some evidence that the positive effect of highly qualified teachers, as measured by the selectivity of the higher education institution they attended, degrees, and test scores, is more pronounced for minority and disadvantaged students. However, the limited research regarding the different types of students and different subject areas precludes definitive conclusions about how specific teacher qualifications vary across these dimensions. This literature review demonstrates that it is inappropriate and potentially misleading to draw generalizations about the effect of teacher attributes across levels of education, subject areas, and types of students.

While this literature review sheds light on the degree to which various teacher attributes typically assumed to reflect teacher quality really do measure teacher effectiveness, its power and persuasiveness is limited by several caveats. First, the meaning of many of the teacher attributes studied in this body of research varies greatly across time and place. For instance, certification involves different requirements in different states.

Teacher education programs vary across institutions in terms of requirements and expectations. Similarly, the pedagogical and subject-matter courses that teachers take in different preparation programs include different content. This idea of "varied treatments" undermines the ability to draw general conclusions about what exactly matters in terms of teacher preparation.

Second, the conclusions drawn here are largely based on the reported statistical significance of estimates resulting from empirical research. However, these general conclusions reveal nothing about the size of the effects. Statistical significance tells us how confident we are that the effect is not zero. Typically, analysts agree that an effect exists so long as it passes a 95% level of confidence; i.e., it is observable at least 95% of the time. While this information is important, it tells us nothing about the magnitude of the effect. An effect that is statistically significant could also be trivial in size, limiting its policy relevance. It is particularly important to take effect size into consideration when making decisions about how to invest a limited stock of resources. Questions relating to whether an intervention is worth the investment can be answered only with good information on the size of the effect and the magnitude of the cost. Further, decisions about competing alternative courses of action require information on relative effect sizes. Policy research on the *quantity* of teachers (i.e., class size) has begun to consider this issue[21]—so should policy research on teacher *quality*.

Finally, and perhaps most importantly, the conclusions presented here should be understood in light of the research that has not been conducted. This literature review reveals several significant gaps in knowledge about the relationship between teacher characteristics and their effectiveness. In particular, greater attention should be devoted to gaining a clearer understanding of elementary education, as well as subjects other than mathematics and science at the secondary level. With respect to teacher certification, degree level, and coursework, most of the definitive findings presented here pertain only to secondary-level mathematics and, to a lesser degree, science. Further, while this review identified some evidence that teacher quality matters most for disadvantaged and minority students, more research is needed to fully understand the specific attributes that make teachers most successful with various types of students.

Implications for policy

Where does all of this information leave us? What do we know about teacher quality, and what are the implications for policy and research? This literature review suggests three implications for policy that should be further explored by policy makers.

1. **Teacher quality is important.** Each year more money is devoted to teacher compensation that to any other category of educational spending. This is consistent with the general agreement among education leaders, policy makers, researchers, and the general public that better teachers lead to better learning. Indeed, empirical research has shown teachers to be the most influential institutional variable in producing student learning—students assigned to high-quality teachers learn more, all other variables being equal. Further, high-quality teachers, as measured by the selectivity of the higher education institution they attended, degrees attained, and test scores, are most important for minority and disadvantaged students. Given the high costs coupled with the high impact of teachers, this educational input has profound implications for the efficiency, equity, and adequacy of public education.

2. **While some current teacher policies and practices are supported by the research, many are based on thin evidence, or no evidence at all.** There is general agreement that teacher quality matters, but the specific definition of teacher quality is the object of much debate. One prevailing conception is that qualifications are important. Take, for instance, the 2002 annual Phi Delta Kappa/Gallup poll of the public's attitudes toward the public schools. An overwhelming majority of respondents believe that teachers should be licensed in the subjects they teach (96%) and that they should pass a competency test before being hired (96%). Existing research provides some direction about which qualifications are actually related to teacher effectiveness. Policy based on evidence from the research would place greater emphasis on subject-specific pedagogical preparation and credentials and teacher test scores shown to be associated with student performance, while de-emphasizing factors like undifferentiated course credits and advanced degrees. It is important to recognize, however, that most of the available evidence focuses on high school mathematics and science. The research on the elementary level of schooling and on subjects other than mathematics and science at the high school level is far more limited.

3. **Teacher policy should reflect an appropriate balance between "professionalization" and "deregulation."** The teacher-reform discourse has been characterized as a polarized debate with those seeking to professionalize teaching on one side and those pushing for deregulation of the profession on the other (Cochran-Smith and Fries 2001). The "professionalizers" argue for higher standards for teach-

ers and a stronger system of credential monitoring to ensure that those entering the profession are of high quality. In contrast, the "deregulators" contend that the current system not only falls short of promoting teacher quality, but actually depletes the potential supply of good teachers by creating unnecessary barriers to the profession. This contingency argues for greater reliance on competency tests rather than more conventional certification or degree programs as the gatekeepers to the profession; given the current professional standards, "deregulators" also support alternative approaches to certification.

The findings from the literature imply that perhaps the most reasonable approach is an appropriate balance between these two extremes. For example, teacher preparation matters, but could occur through traditional colleges of education as well as through proven alternative routes. Further, schools of education can coexist and share the responsibility for preparing teachers with academic departments, given the demonstrated importance of both kinds of coursework and knowledge. Likewise, both sides of the debate seem to agree, and the empirical evidence confirms, that teacher assessments may be a useful tool for identifying, rewarding, and distributing high-quality teachers. Cochran-Smith and Fries (2001) are correct in their assessment that much of the debate over teacher policy is fueled by a highly political climate that has stratified the discourse. Nonetheless, the empirical evidence suggests some reasonable courses of action that could be simultaneously consistent with both sides of the debate. Any possibility of progress must involve a reasonable, evidence-based discussion and a willingness on both sides to compromise in the interest of students in all schools.

The evidence reviewed here provides some clarity about what is known about characteristics indicative of teacher quality. Addressing the issue of teacher quality demands sensitivity to the complexity of the problem, awareness of the contextual circumstances of individual schools and school systems wrestling with the challenge of attracting and keeping good teachers, and an understanding of the necessity for the high price tag associated with staffing *every* classroom—even the most challenging ones—with high-quality teachers.

Endnotes

1. The 1999-2000 NCES information is based on projected or preliminary data.

2. Of course, to the degree that reduced class sizes, overall educational spending, and teacher salaries are related to teacher quality, these can be viewed as investments in teacher quality, albeit indirect.

3. Rivkin, Hanushek, and Kain (1998) identify teachers as a major determinant of student performance, but do not describe teacher quality in terms of specific qualifications and characteristics. They show strong, systematic differences in expected achievement gains related to different teachers using a variance-components model.

4. Some have challenged the degree to which research supports the recommendations made by NCFAF. See Ballou & Podgursky (1997, 1999, 2000) and, for a rebuttal, Darling-Hammond (2000).

5. Some argue that the qualifications identified in the NCLB legislation are more reflective of a "minimally qualified teacher" than a "highly qualified teacher."

6. In contrast to many of the policy recommendations for stricter teacher qualifications, the Abell Foundation has recently released a report calling for the elimination of statewide coursework and certification requirements for teachers in favor of more flexible professional requirements (Abell Foundation 2001). Likewise, Hess (2002) argues for the deregulation of teacher preparation.

7. It was not enough for a study to simply include a teacher attribute as a control variable. Rather, a policy-relevant teacher attribute, often assumed by policy makers as well as the general public to reflect teacher quality, had to be a key independent variable in the study.

8. However, the variability in quality remains considerable. This review outlines study designs and assigns greater weight to more rigorous designs in the conclusions drawn.

9. The quality of the institution attended could be viewed as a proxy for the quality of the experience.

10. Of course, most teacher hiring decisions are not only based on measurable qualifications such as certification, but also on principals' subjective judgments that have much to do with teachers' personalities.

11. The author acknowledges Whitney Allgood for her contributions to this section.

12. Here and elsewhere in this document, the term "nationally representative" describes the data set used for particular studies. However, the samples used by researchers are not necessarily nationally representative.

13. High School and Beyond (HS&B) is a stratified national probability sample of over 1,100 secondary schools with up to 36 sophomores and 36 seniors initially

interviewed from each school in the spring of 1980. Over 30,000 sophomores and 28,000 seniors participated in the base year interviews. The HS&B sample describes the activities of seniors and sophomores as they progressed through high school, postsecondary education, and into the workplace. The data span 1980 through 1992 and include parent, teacher, high school transcripts, student financial aid records, and postsecondary transcripts in addition to student questionnaires, interviews, and test scores.

14. The Longitudinal Study of American Youth (LSAY) is a panel survey of American public middle and high school science and mathematics education. The first data collection occurred in the fall of 1987. The older LSAY cohort consisted of a national sample of approximately 3,000 tenth-grade students in public high schools throughout the United States. These students were eventually followed for a period of seven years, ending four years after high school, with some students just finishing a baccalaureate degree while others were employed, raising a family, or serving in the military. The younger LSAY cohort consisted of a national sample of approximately 3,000 seventh-grade students in public schools that served as feeder schools to the same high schools in which the older cohort was enrolled. These students were followed through the end of their high school years and were interviewed approximately one year after the end of high school. Survey instruments were completed by the sampled students, their teachers, their principal, and their parents. In addition, achievement tests focused on mathematics and science knowledge were administered in the fall of each year students were in school.

15. *Prospects: The Congressionally Mandated Study of Educational Opportunity* contains a longitudinal study of public-school students. This dataset is designed to assess the students' academic achievement and other measures of school success. It consists of a nationally representative sample of students in the three grade cohorts, along with their parents, teachers, and principals.

The researchers caution that the *Prospects* data include only a small number of teachers who had subject-specific degrees or special certification to teach math or reading.

16. The National Educational Longitudinal Survey (NELS:88) is a panel study designed to provide trend data about critical transitions experienced by young people as they develop, attend school, and embark on their careers. The base year of the survey collected in 1988 included 24,599 eighth-grade students attending roughly 1,000 randomly selected middle schools. Researchers followed approximately 12,000 of these eighth-grade students into 1,200 public and private high schools. Data were collected from students and their parents, teachers, and high school principals and from existing school records such as high school transcripts. Cognitive tests (math, science, reading, and history) were administered during the base year (1988), first follow up (1990), and second follow up (1992). Third follow up data were collected in 1994. All dropouts who could be located were retained in the study.

17. If emergency certified teachers are movers who were fully certified elsewhere, then it seems that both Darling-Hammond, et al. and Goldhaber and Brewer are correct: the teachers are fully prepared, but the formal training required for this preparation may be different from what the teachers in the current district who hold standard certification have experienced.

18. The interns in this study are individuals in the alternative teacher preparation program who are completing the required one-year internship teaching in the schools with supervision by a mentor and the school district.

19. Of course, the value of any test as an indicator of teacher quality depends on the predictive validity of the test. In other words, some tests are more reflective of the kinds of skills and knowledge that teachers need to do their jobs well.

20. The NELS:88 teacher survey included a single item designed to measure teachers' knowledge of mathematics. The test score variable used in this study was a value of 1 if the teacher answered the item correctly, and 0 if the teacher answered it incorrectly.

21. For example, see Krueger (2002).

Bibliography

Abell Foundation. 2001. *Teacher Certification Reconsidered: Stumbling for Quality.* Baltimore: Abell Foundation.

Adams, P. E. and G. H. Krockover. 1997. Beginning science teacher cognition and its origins in the pre-service science teacher program. *Journal of Research in Science Teaching.* Vol. 34, pp. 633-53.

Allgood, W. and J. K. Rice. 2002. "The Adequacy of Urban Education: Focusing on Teacher Quality." In C. F. Roellke and J. K. Rice, eds., *Fiscal Policy Issues in Urban Education.* Greenwich, Conn.: Information Age Publishing, Inc., pp. 155-80

Andrew, M. D. 1990. Differences between graduates of 4-year and 5-year teacher preparation programs. *Journal of Teacher Education.* Vol. 41, pp. 45-51.

Andrew, M. D. and R. L. Schwab. 1995. Has reform in teacher education influenced teacher performance? An outcome assessment of graduates of eleven teacher education programs. *Action in Teacher Education.* Vol. 17, No. 3, pp. 43-54.

Andrews, J. W., C. R. Blackmon, and J. A. Mackey. 1980. Pre-service performance and the National Teacher Exams. *Phi Delta Kappan.* Vol. 61, No. 5, pp. 358-59.

Ashton, P. and L. Crocker. 1987. Systematic study of planned variations: The essential focus of teacher education reform. *Journal of Teacher Education.* Vol. 38, No. 3, pp. 2-8.

Ayers, J. B. 1988. Another look at the concurrent and predictive validity of the national teacher examinations. *Journal of Educational Research.* Vol. 81, No. 3, pp. 133-37.

Ayers, J. B., and G. S. Qualls. 1979. Concurrent and predictive validity of the National Teacher Examinations. *Journal of Educational Research.* Vol. 73, No. 2, pp. 86-91.

Ballou, D. and M. Podgursky. 2000. Reforming teacher preparation and licensing: Continuing the debate. *Teachers College Record.* Vol. 102, No.1, pp. 5-27.

Ballou, D. and M. Podgursky. 1997. Reforming teacher training and recruitment: A critical appraisal of the recommendations of NCTAF. *Government Union Review.* Vol. 17, No. 4.

Boyer, E. 1983. *High School.* Menlo Park, CA: Carnegie Foundation for the Advancement of Teaching.

Bush, R. N. 1987. Teacher education reform: Lessons from the past half century. *Journal of Teacher Education.* Vol. 38, No. 3, pp. 13-19.

Clark, D. C., R. B. Smith., T. J. Newby, and V. A. Cook. 1985. Perceived origins of teaching behavior. *Journal of Teacher Education.* Vol. 36, No. 6, pp. 49-53.

Clift, R. 1991. Learning to teach English—maybe: A study of knowledge development. *Journal of Teacher Education*. Vol. 42, pp. 357-72.

Cochran-Smith, M. and M. K. Fries. 2001. Sticks, stones, and ideology: The discourse of reform in teacher education. *Educational Researcher*. Vol. 30, No. 8, pp. 3-15.

Darling-Hammond, L. 2000. Teacher quality and student achievement: A review of state policy evidence. *Journal of Education Policy Analysis*. Vol. 8, No. 1.

Darling-Hammond, L. 1990. Teaching and knowledge: Policy issues posed by alternate certification for teachers. *Peabody Journal of Education*. Vol. 67, No. 3, pp. 123-54.

Darling-Hammond, L., B. Berry, and A. Thoreson. 2001. Does teacher certification matter? Evaluating the evidence. *Educational Evaluation and Policy Analysis*. Vol. 23, No. 1, pp. 57-77.

Dewalt, M. and D. W. Ball. 1987. Some effects of training on the competence of beginning teachers. *Journal of Educational Research*. Vol. 80, No. 6, pp. 343-47.

Dorby, A. M., P. D. Murphy, and D. M. Schmidt. 1985. Predicting teacher competence. *Action in Teacher Education*. Vol. 7, Nos. 1-2, pp. 69-74.

Druva, C. A. and R. D. Anderson. 1983. Science teacher characteristics by teacher behavior and by student outcome: A meta-analysis of research. *Journal of Research in Science Teaching*. Vol. 20, No. 5, pp. 467-79.

Eberts, R. W. and J. A. Stone. 1984. *Unions and Public Schools*. Lexington, Mass.: D.C. Heath and Company.

Ehrenberg, R. G. and D. J. Brewer. 1995. Did teachers' verbal ability and race matter in the 1960s? *Coleman* revisited. *Economics of Education Review*. Vol. 14, No. 1, pp. 1-21.

Ehrenberg, R. G. and D. J. Brewer. 1994. Do school and teacher characteristics matter? Evidence from high school and beyond. *Economics of Education Review*. Vol. 13, No.1, pp. 1-17.

Eisenhart, M., L. Behm, and L. Romagnano. 1991. Learning to teach: Developing expertise or rite of passage? *Journal of Education for Teaching*. Vol. 17, pp. 51-71.

Evertson, C. M., W. D. Hawley, and M. Zlotnik. 1985. Making a difference in educational quality through teacher education. *Journal of Teacher Education*. Vol. 36, No. 3, pp. 2-12.

Ferguson, R. F. 1998. "Can Schools Narrow the Black-White Test Score Gap?" In C. Jencks and M. Phillips, eds., *The Black-White Test Score Gap*. Washington, D.C.: Brookings.

Ferguson, R. F. 1991. Paying for public education: New evidence on how and why money matters. *Harvard Journal of Legislation*. Vol. 28, pp. 465-98.

Ferguson, R. F. and H. F. Ladd. 1996. "How and Why Money Matters: An Analysis of Alabama Schools." In H. F. Ladd, ed., *Holding Schools Accountable: Performance-Based Reform in Education*. Washington, D.C.: Brookings.

Ferguson, R. F. and S. T. Womack. 1993. The impact of subject matter and education coursework on teaching performance. *Journal of Teacher Education.* Vol. 44, No. 1, pp. 55-63.

Fideler, E. F., E. D. Foster, and S. Schwartz. 2000. *The Urban Teacher Challenge: Teacher Demand and Supply in the Great City Schools.* Belmont, MA: Urban Teacher Collaborative. < http://www.cgcs.org/pdfs/utc.pdf >

Goldhaber, D. D. and D. J. Brewer. 2001. Evaluating the evidence on teacher certification: A rejoinder. *Educational Evaluation and Policy Analysis.* Vol. 23, No. 1, pp. 79-86.

Goldhaber, D. D. and D. J. Brewer. 2000. Does teacher certification matter? High school teacher certification status and student achievement. *Educational Evaluation and Policy Analysis.* Vol. 22, No. 2, 129-46.

Goldhaber, D. D. and D. J. Brewer. 1998. When should we reward degrees for teachers? *Phi Delta Kappan.* Vol. 80, No. 2, pp. 134-38.

Goldhaber, D. D. and D. J. Brewer. 1997. Why don't schools and teachers seem to matter? Assessing the impact of unobservables on educational productivity. *The Journal of Human Resources.* Vol. 32, No. 3, pp. 505-23.

Goodman, J. 1985. What students learn from early field experience: A case study and critical analysis. *Journal of Teacher Education.* Vol. 36, No. 6, pp. 42-8.

Greenwald, R., L. V. Hedges, and R. D. Laine. 1996. The effect of school resources on student achievement. *Review of Educational Research.* Vol. 66, No. 3, pp. 361-96.

Griffin, G. A. 1989. A descriptive study of student teaching. *Elementary School Journal.* Vol. 89, pp. 343-64.

Grissmer, D., A. Flanagan, J. Kawata, S. Williamson. 2000. *Improving Student Achievement: What State NAEP Scores Tell Us.* Arlington, Va.: RAND.

Grossman, P. L. 1989. Learning to teach without teacher education. *Teachers College Record.* Vol. 91, pp. 191-207.

Grossman, P. L. and A. E. Richert. 1988. Unacknowledged knowledge growth: A re-examination of the effects of teacher education. *Teaching and Teacher Education.* Vol. 4, pp. 53-62.

Grossman, P. L., S. Valencia, K. Evans, C. Thompson, S. Martin, and N. Place. 2003. Transitions into teaching: Learning to teach writing in teacher education and beyond. Center on English Learning and Achievement. < http://cela.albany.edu/transitions/main.html >

Guthrie, J. W. and R. Rothstein. 2001. "A New Millennium and a Likely New Era of Education Finance." In S. Chaikind and W.J. Fowler, eds., *Education Finance in the New Millennium.* Larchmont, N.Y.: Eye on Education.

Guyton, E. and E. Farokhi. 1987. Relationships among academic performance, basic skills, subject matter knowledge, and teaching skills of teacher education graduates. *Journal of Teacher Education.* Vol. 38, No. 5, pp. 37-42.

Guyton, E., M. C. Fox, and K. A. Sisk. 1991. Comparisons of teaching attitudes, teacher efficacy, and teacher performance of first-year teachers prepared by alternative and traditional teacher education programs. *Action in Teacher Education.* Vol. 13, No. 2, pp. 1-9.

Hanushek, E. A. 1997. Assessing the effects of school resources on student performance: An update. *Educational Evaluation and Policy Analysis.* Vol. 19, No. 2, pp. 141-64.

Hanushek, E. A. 1996. "School Resources and Student Performance." In Burtless, Gary, ed., *Does Money Matter: The Effect of School Resources on Student Achievement and Adult Success.* Washington, D.C.: Brookings

Hanushek, E. A. 1986. The economics of schooling: Production and efficiency in public schools. *Journal of Economic Literature,* Vol. 24, pp. 1141-77.

Hanushek, E. A. 1981. Throwing money at schools. *Journal of Policy Analysis and Management.* Vol. 1, No. 10, pp. 19-41.

Hanushek, E.A., J. F. Kain, and S. G. Rivkin. 1998. "Teachers, Schools, and Academic Achievement." NBER Working Paper No. 6691. < http://www.nber.org/papers/w6691 >

Hanushek, E. A., J. F. Kain, and S. G. Rivkin. 1999. "Do higher salaries buy better teachers?" National Bureau of Economic Research Working Paper No. 7082. < http://www.nber.org/papers/w7082 >

Harnisch, D. L. 1987. Characteristics associated with effective public high schools. *Journal of Educational Research.* Vol. 80, pp. 233-41.

Hawk, P. P., C. R. Coble, and M. Swanson. 1985. Certification: It does matter. *Journal of Teacher Education.* Vol. 36, No. 3, pp. 13-15.

Hawk, P. P. and M. W. Schmidt. 1989. Teacher preparation: A comparison of traditional and alternative programs. *Journal of Teacher Education.* Vol. 40, No. 5, pp. 53-8.

Hawley, W. D. 1987. The high costs and doubtful efficacy of extended teach-preparation programs: An invitation to more basic reforms. *American Journal of Education.* Vol. 95, No. 2, pp. 275-98.

Hawley, W. D. 1990. The theory and practice of alternative certification: Implications for the improvement of teaching. *Peabody Journal of Education.* Vol. 67, No. 3, pp. 3-34.

Haycock, K. 2000. Honor in the boxcar: Equalizing teacher quality. *Thinking K-16.* Vol. 4, No. 1.

Hedges, L. V., R. D. Laine, and R. Greenwald. 1994a. Does money matter? A meta-analysis of studies of the effects of differential school inputs on student outcomes. *Educational Researcher.* Vol. 23, No. 3, pp. 5-14.

Hedges, L. V., R. D. Laine, and R. Greenwald. 1994b. Money does matter somewhere: A reply to Hanushek. *Educational Researcher.* Vol. 23, No.4, pp. 9-10.

Hess, F. M. 2002. Break the link. *Education Next.* Vol. 2, No. 1, pp. 22-28.

Hollingsworth, S. 1989. Prior beliefs and cognitive change in learning to teach. *American Educational Research Journal.* Vol. 26, pp. 160-89.

Holmes Group. 1986. *Tomorrow's Teachers: A Report of the Holmes Group.* East Lansing, Mich.: Holmes Group.

Kennedy, M. M. 1999. "The Problem of Evidence in Teacher Education." In R.A. Roth, ed., *The Role of the University in the Preparation of Teachers.* Philadelphia, Pa.: Falmer.

Kennedy, M. M. 1996. *Research Genres in Teacher Education.* In F. Murray, ed., *The Teacher Educator's Handbook: Building a Knowledge Base for the Preparation of Teachers.* San Francisco, Calif.: Jossey Bass.

Kiesling, H. J. 1984. Assignment practices and the relationship of instructional time to the reading performance of elementary school children. *Economics of Education Review.* Vol. 3, No. 4, pp. 341-50.

Krueger, A. 2002. "Understanding the Magnitude and Effect of Class Size on Student Achievement." In L. Mishel and R. Rothstein, eds., *The Class Size Debate.* Washington, D.C.: Economic Policy Institute.

Latham, A. S., D. Gitomer, and R. Ziomek. 1999. What the tests tell us about new teachers. *Educational Leadership.* Vol. 56, No. 8, pp. 23-6.

Lawrenz, F. 1975. The relationship between science teacher characteristics and student achievement and attitude. *Journal of Research in Science Teaching.* Vol. 12, No. 4, pp. 433-37.

Link, C. R and E. C. Ratledge. 1979. Student perceptions, I.Q., and achievement. *Journal of Human Resources.* Vol. 14, pp. 98-111.

Lutz, F. W. and J. B. Hutton. 1989. Alternative teacher certification: Its policy implications for classroom and personnel practice. *Educational Evaluation and Policy Analysis.* Vol. 11, No. 3, pp. 237-54.

Mayer, D. P., J. E. Mullens, M. T. Moore, and J. Ralph. 2000. *Monitoring School Quality: An Indicators Report.* Washington, D.C.: U.S. Department of Education.

McDiarmid, G. W. and S. M. Wilson. 1991. An exploration of the subject matter knowledge of alternate route teachers: Can we assume they know their subject. *Journal of Teacher Education.* Vol. 42, No. 2, pp. 93-103.

Miller, J. W., M. C. McKenna, and B.A. McKenna. 1998. A comparison of alternatively and traditionally prepared teachers. *Journal of Teacher Education.* Vol. 49, No. 3, 165-76.

Monk, D. H. 1994. Subject area preparation of secondary mathematics and science teachers and student achievement. *Economics of Education Review.* Vol. 13, No. 2, pp. 125-45.

Monk, D. H. and J. A. King. 1994. "Multilevel Teacher Resource Effects in Pupil Performance in Secondary Mathematics and Science: The Case of Teacher Subject-Matter Preparation." In R.G. Ehrenberg, ed., *Choices and Consequences: Contemporary Policy Issues in Education.* Ithaca, N.Y.: ILR Press.

Murnane, R. J. and B. R. Phillips. 1981. What do effective teachers of inner-city children have in common? *Social Science Research.* Vol. 10, pp. 83-100.

National Center for Education Statistics. 2000. *Digest of Education Statistics, 2000.* Washington, D.C.: U.S. Department of Education, Office of Educational Research and Improvement.

National Commission on Excellence in Education. 1983. *A Nation at Risk.* Washington, D.C.: NCEE.

National Commission on Teaching and America's Future. 1996. *What Matters Most: Teaching for America's Future.* New York: National Commission on Teaching and America's Future.

National Research Council. 2001 *Testing Teacher Candidates: The Role of Licensure Tests in Improving Teacher Quality.* Committee on Assessment and Teacher Quality. Mitchell, K.J., Robinson, D.Z., Plake, B.S., and Knowles, K.T., editors. Board on Testing and Assessment, Center for Education, Division of Behavioral and Social Sciences and Education. Washington, D.C.: National Academy Press.

Nelson, B. and L. Wood. 1985. The competency dilemma. *Action in Teacher Education.* Vol. 7, Nos. 1-2, pp. 45-58.

Odden, A. and C. Kelley. 2002. *Paying Teachers for What They Know and Can Do: New and Smarter Compensation Strategies to Improve Schools.* Thousand Oaks, Calif.: Corwin Press.

Perkes, V. A. 1967-68. Junior high school science teacher preparation, teaching behavior, and student achievement. *Journal of Research in Science Teaching.* Vol. 5, pp. 121-26.

Phillips, M., J. Crouse, and J. Ralph. 1998. "Does the Black-White Test Score Gap Widen After Children Enter School?" In Phillips and Crouse, eds., *The Black-White Test Score Gap.* Washington, D.C.: Brookings Institution Press.

Pigge, F. L. 1978. Teacher competencies: Need, proficiency, and where proficiency was developed. *Journal of Teacher Education.* Vol. 29, No. 4, pp. 70-6.

Piper, M. K. and P. S. O'Sullivan. 1981. The national teacher examination: Can it predict classroom performance? *Phi Delta Kappan.* Vol. 62, No. 5, pp. 401.

Prince, C.D. 2002. *The Challenges of Attracting Good Teachers and Principals to Struggling Schools.* Arlington, Va.: American Association of School Administrators.

Quirk, T. J., B. J. Witten, and S. F. Weinberg. 1973. Review of studies of the concurrent and predictive validity of the National Teacher Examinations. *Review of Educational Research.* Vol. 43, No. 1, pp. 89-113.

Rivkin, S. G., E. A. Hanushek, and J. F. Kain. 1998. "Teachers, schools, and academic achievement." National Bureau of Economic Research, Working Paper 6691.

Rowan, B., R. Correnti, and R. J. Miller. 2002. What large-scale, survey research tells us about teacher effects on student achievement: Insights from the *Prospects* student of elementary schools. *Teachers College Record.* Vol. 104, No. 8, pp. 1525-67.

Rowan, B., F. Chiang, and R. J. Miller. 1997. Using research on employees' performance to study the effects of teachers on students' achievement. *Sociology of Education.* Vol. 70, October, pp. 256-84.

Sanders, W. L. 1998. Value-added assessment. *The School Administrator.* Vol. 55, No. 11, 24-32.

Sanders, W. L. and J. C. Rivers. 1996. *Cumulative and Residual Effects of Teachers on Future Academic Achievement.* University of Tennessee Value-Added Research and Assessment Center.

Sandham, J. L. November 18, 2000. State teacher-bonus plan catches Florida districts short. *Education Week.* pp. 25, 27.

Shulman, J. 1987. From veteran parent to novice teacher: A case study of a student teacher. *Teaching and Teacher Education.* Vol. 3, pp. 13-27.

Sheehan, D. S. and M. Marcus. 1978. Teacher performance on national teacher examinations and student mathematics and vocabulary achievement. *Journal of Educational Research.* Vol. 71, No. 3, pp. 134-36.

Silvernail, D. L. and M. H. Costello. 1983. The impact of student teaching and internship programs on preservice teachers' pupil control perspectives, anxiety levels, and teaching concerns. *Journal of Teacher Education.* Vol. 33, No. 4, pp. 32-6.

Speakman, S. T., B. Cooper, R. Sampiere, J. May, H. Holsomback, and B. Glass. 1996. "Bringing Dollars to the Classroom." In L.O. Picus and L. Wattenbarger, eds., *Where Does the Money Go? Resource Allocation in Elementary and Secondary Schools.* Thousand Oaks, Calif.: Corwin.

Stafford, D. and G. Barrow. 1994. Houston's alternative certification program. *Educational Forum.* Vol. 58, pp. 193-8.

Stedman, C. H. 1984. Testing for competency: A pyrrhic victory? *Journal of Teacher Education.* Vol. 35, No. 2, pp. 2-5.

Strauss, R. P. and E. A. Sawyer. 1986. Some new evidence on teacher and student competencies. *Economics of Education Review.* Vol. 5, No. 1, pp. 41-8.

Summers, A. A. and B. L. Wolfe. 1975. *Equality of Educational Opportunity Quantified: A Production Function Approach.* Philadelphia, Pa.: Federal Reserve Bank of Philadelphia.

Summers, A. A. and B.L. Wolfe. 1977. Do schools make a difference? *American Economic Review.* Vol. 67, pp. 639-52.

Turner, S.E. 1998. "The training of teachers: The changing degree output in the area of education." Paper presented at the annual meeting of the Association of Public Policy and Management, New York, N.Y.

Wayne, A. J. and P. Youngs. 2003. Teacher characteristics and student achievement gains: A review. *Review of Educational Research.* Vol. 73, No. 1, pp. 89-122.

Whitehurst, G. J. 2002. "Scientifically based research on teacher quality: Research on teacher preparation and professional development." Paper presented at the White House Conference on Preparing Tomorrow's Teachers. March 5, 2002.

Wilson, S. M., R. E. Floden, and J. Ferrini-Mundy. 2001. *Teacher Preparation Research: Current Knowledge, Gaps, and Recommendations.* Seattle, Wash.: Center for the Study of Teaching and Policy.